00027696

320.943 FAI

A2
US & Comparative Government & Politics

Paul Fairclough

Coleg Sir Gâr
Canolfan Ddysgu
Llanelli
Learning Centre

D0315519

COLEG SIR GAR

Dawson	7.9.08
	8.99

Philip Allan Updates
Market Place
Deddington
Oxfordshire
OX15 0SE

Orders

Bookpoint Ltd, 130 Milton Park, Abingdon, Oxfordshire, OX14 4SB
tel: 01235 827720
fax: 01235 400454
e-mail: uk.orders@bookpoint.co.uk
Lines are open 9.00 a.m.–5.00 p.m., Monday to Saturday, with a 24-hour message answering service. You can also order through the Philip Allan Updates website: www.philipallan.co.uk

© Philip Allan Updates 2004

ISBN-13: 978-0-86003-763-7
ISBN-10: 0-86003-763-0

All rights reserved; no part of this publication may be reproduced, stored in a retrieval system, or transmitted, in any form or by any means, electronic, mechanical, photocopying, recording or otherwise without either the prior written permission of Philip Allan Updates or a licence permitting restricted copying in the United Kingdom issued by the Copyright Licensing Agency Ltd, 90 Tottenham Court Road, London W1T 4LP.

Printed in Malta

Philip Allan Updates' policy is to use papers that are natural, renewable and recyclable products and made from wood grown in sustainable forests. The logging and manufacturing processes are expected to conform to the environmental regulations of the country of origin.

Contents

Introduction

US Government and Politics: Questions and Answers

Comparative Government and Politics: Questions and Answers

Introduction

This question and answer guide has been written as a companion for students carrying on their studies beyond AS to A2. It is aimed specifically at those candidates who are following the US route of any of the three Government and Politics specifications — AQA, Edexcel or OCR.

This book provides exam-style questions and possible answers that cover 16 topic areas, and in each area two or more questions of varying type are considered. Though the style of examination questions varies somewhat from board to board, there is enough common ground across the three specifications for most questions to be of use to all students.

How to use this guide

As is the case with any study aid, this guide is aimed at helping you to develop your work. It is a good idea to attempt the questions provided here without first reading the student answers. Once you have done this, you can review your own work in light of the examiner's advice and comments provided. Remember that these student answers are not model answers for you to learn and reproduce word-for-word in the examination. It is unlikely that the questions in the examination will be worded exactly as they are here and, in any case, there is always more than one way of answering any question effectively.

Knowing your specification

It is important to familiarise yourself with the main elements of the specification that you are studying — the content for each module and the format of the examination. Specifically, you should know:
- the number of questions on each paper
- how much choice you will have on each paper
- the type of questions that you will face

In order to do this you need to have a copy of the subject specification. Your teacher may have given this to you at the start of the course. It is important to refer to it because it tells you what the examiners expect you to know. If you cannot get this information from your teacher, look on your examination board's website:
- **www.aqa.org.uk**
- **www.edexcel.org.uk**
- **www.ocr.org.uk**

On each of these sites there are complete downloadable copies of each board's specification and sample papers. These papers enable you to familiarise yourself with the type of questions you can expect in the examination. Your board may also produce a Teachers' Guide which will give you extra information about what you need to know for the examination. The table below outlines the modules that you will be studying if you follow the US route at A2.

	AQA	Edexcel	OCR
Module 4	Comparative UK/US Government	Representation in the US	US Government and Politics
Module 5	Politics of the USA	Governing the USA	Government and Politics Research*
Module 6	Synoptic	Comparative UK and US Politics	Government and Politics (US Option)

*either coursework or written examination

Assessment Objectives

You should be aware of the three Assessment Objectives (AOs), which are common to all three Government and Politics specifications. The weighting for each varies according to the individual specifications for each board, but the general principles, as outlined by the Qualifications and Curriculum Authority (QCA), are as follows:

AO	Requirement	Weighting
AO1	recall, select and deploy knowledge of Government and Politics accurately, showing understanding of relevant political concepts and theories	40–50%
AO2	analyse and evaluate political information, arguments and explanations, and identify parallels, connections, similarities and differences between aspects of the political systems studied	30–40%
AO3	communicate arguments and explanations in a clear and structured manner, making use of a range of relevant evidence and appropriate political vocabulary	10–20%

QCA also provides generic descriptors for grades A, C and E. These descriptors specify exactly what is required at each level.

Grade A	• a comprehensive knowledge of political institutions and processes and the relationships between them, demonstrating excellent contextual awareness
	• detailed and comprehensive interpretations or explanations
	• accurate evidence and up-to-date examples
	• a wide range of well-developed concepts and theories, using appropriate political vocabulary
	• a sophisticated awareness of differing viewpoints and a clear recognition of issues
	• identification of parallels and connections together with well-developed comparisons

Grade A	• a clear and full evaluation of political institutions, processes, behaviour, arguments or explanations • clear communication of arguments, explanations and conclusions • a conclusion that flows from the discussion
Grade C	• sound knowledge of political institutions and processes and the relationships between them, demonstrating sound contextual awareness • developed and effective interpretations or explanations • clear evidence backed up by good examples • a range of developed concepts and theories, using political vocabulary • an awareness of differing viewpoints and a recognition of issues • recognition of parallels and connections together with some comparisons • good evaluation of political institutions, processes, behaviour, arguments or explanations • good communication of arguments, explanations and conclusions • a conclusion clearly linked to the preceding discussion
Grade E	• an outline knowledge of political institutions and processes and some relationships between them, demonstrating contextual awareness covering part of the question • a partial but reasonably effective attempt at interpretation or explanation • some not very detailed examples • a limited range of concepts and theories • limited analysis that shows some awareness of differing viewpoints • a recognition of basic parallels and connections together with limited comparisons • a simple attempt to evaluate political institutions, processes, behaviour, arguments or explanations • adequate communication of arguments and conclusions • a conclusion with modest or implicit relationship to the preceding discussion

Source: www.qca.org.uk

Question format

The precise format of the questions in the A2 examinations depends largely on the specification, but all three specifications require you to produce an extended essay. These essays will be longer than anything that you had to write in your AS Politics examinations.

AQA questions

If you are following the AQA specification, you should be aware that the Module 4 and 5 examinations (GOV4 and GOV5) are each $1\frac{1}{2}$ hours long. Each paper requires you to answer a compulsory three-part question (total 40 marks) plus *one* of a choice of three traditional essay-type questions (again worth 40 marks). The three-part questions are based around an extract:

- part (a) (8 marks) normally asks you to explain what is meant by a specified term
- part (b) (12 marks) requires you to use your own knowledge as well as the extract to deal with some specified aspect of the topic
- part (c) (20 marks) is essentially a 'mini-essay', normally addressing a broader aspect of the topic

It is vital that you remember that Module 4 (GOV4) is a comparative paper and you must therefore compare the UK and the USA at all times *explicitly*, even if the questions do not tell you to.

Edexcel questions
If you are following Edexcel route C (USA), you will find that Modules 4 and 5 (6500 and 6501) are similar in format to one another. Each paper is $1\frac{1}{4}$ hours long and is divided into two sections. In the first section you must answer one 15-minute single-part short-answer question (20 marks) from a choice of four. In the second section you must answer one 45-minute traditional essay question (60 marks) from a choice of three. Module 6C (6502) is $1\frac{1}{2}$ hours long and you are required to answer two traditional 45-minute essay questions (50 marks each) from a choice of four.

OCR questions
OCR Modules 4 (2694) and 6 (2698) are each $1\frac{1}{2}$ hours long. Module 4 requires you to answer three 30-mark traditional essay questions from a choice of eight (30 minutes per question). In Module 6 you have to answer two 60-mark traditional essay questions (45 minutes each). The different paper totals (90 and 120 respectively) reflect the relative weighting of these two modules.

As you can see, the main feature common to all three specifications is the requirement to answer 30–45-minute traditional essay-type questions. As a result, much of this book focuses on such essay questions, though some shorter, definition-based questions are covered too.

Approaching traditional essay questions
The key to producing good extended essay answers at A-level is understanding what the question is asking you to do. Pay close attention to the precise wording of the question in order to ascertain exactly what skills and knowledge you need to demonstrate.

Command phrases
You will be familiar with some of the more common 'command phrases' from your AS examinations and you may still find these phrases or similar ones at A2. Examples include:
- 'Examine/assess the view that...'

- 'Evaluate the effectiveness of...'
- 'What factors determine the...'
- 'Account for the...'
- 'What is the significance of...'
- 'Discuss the role and importance of...'
- 'Assess the claim that...'

In answering such questions it is vital that you keep what you have been asked to do at the centre of your thoughts and at the centre of your answer. Look at the following question:

What factors determine the outcome of votes within Congress?

This question asks you to identify a number of factors that might have an influence on the voting behaviour of those within Congress, either individually or collectively. At the same time, you need to come to a judgement regarding the relative importance of the factors that you have highlighted.

Structure

When answering this question your first step should be to identify those factors that you intend to examine. In the 40 minutes available it is probably realistic to deal with three or four factors comprehensively: fewer than this might result in an answer that lacks balance, while attempting to deal with too many factors might render your response disjointed and superficial. Precisely how much you write on each factor will be determined largely by the speed at which you can write coherently. Allowing half a side per factor, plus an introduction and a conclusion, gives you a fairly typical three-side examination essay.

A typical structure for this type of essay would be:

The same structure can also be applied to essays that do not ask you to identify a range of factors. Decide which three or four areas are central to the title and write out a brief plan so that you don't forget any of them or become side-tracked once you are writing.

Planning out your answer in this way might take 1 or 2 minutes in the examination room. It can be nerve-wracking to take the time to make a plan, especially if everyone around you has already started writing, but it could help you to avoid disasters later on. Unless you want the examiner to mark your plan as part of your answer, you should cross it out neatly when you have finished your essay.

Style and flow

The order in which you deal with factors is important. It may be that one factor leads on naturally from another and you need to give this some thought before you start writing. Dealing with factors in an illogical or random order can affect the flow and fluency of your essay. A logically structured answer is likely to achieve high marks for communication. One way of helping your essay to flow well is to pay close attention to the way in which you move from one factor (i.e. one paragraph) to the next. The careful use of **linking phrases** can give the essay a real sense of direction. Take the 'voting in Congress' title, for example. If Factor 1 was 'party pressure' and Factor 2 was 'constituency pressure', the Factor 2 paragraph could begin with a sentence such as:

> Though a Congressman's party may still have some influence over how he or she votes within Congress — despite the relative weaknesses of party 'whips' within the US legislature — most Congressmen still have to pay far more attention to the attitudes and needs of their constituents.

Using linking phrases helps you to move from one factor to another in a more considered fashion.

Focus

Your answer needs to be focused explicitly on the title from the start. A good way of ensuring this is to employ key phrases and words from the title in your answer. At the same time, you should aim to demonstrate your knowledge and understanding within an analytical framework, rather than simply describing. With practice it is possible to do both of these tasks at the same time. Two methods are given below:

(1) Many commentators [a named commentator would obviously be better] feel that [insert Factor A] is a key factor in **determining** how some Congressmen vote on certain issues because...

(2) While [insert Factor B] may not be as important as [insert Factor A, discussed previously], it clearly has a significant influence on the outlook of many House members representing southern rural districts and this, in turn, plays a part in **determining the outcome of votes within Congress**.

Writing in this way ensures that you stay focused on the title and keep your answer analytical, minimising the chances of losing your way in lengthy descriptive passages.

Attacking a proposition

You may find that some of the longer 45-minute essay questions differ from AS questions, in that they consist of a short quotation followed by a command phrase. For example:

'Some politicians are Republican, some Democratic, and their feud is dramatic, but except for the name they are identically the same' (Ogden Nash). How accurate is this assessment of US political parties?

There are two golden rules to follow when answering questions like this one:

(1) Do not panic about the quotation itself. In the example above you are simply being asked to what extent you agree with the view that US political parties are

indistinguishable from one another, beyond their names. This is a straightforward question that can be phrased in any number of ways. You have probably tackled the same question in some form or another as part of your studies in this subject.

(2) Do not simply accept the sentiment expressed in the quotation without question. Consider the following title:

'Neither the US cabinet nor its UK counterpart has much basis in law, yet they both exert a massive influence on the direction of policy in their respective countries.' How accurate is this view?

Even though the command phrase is asking you to assess the accuracy of the view expressed, the vast majority of candidates will simply use the knowledge that they have to explain why someone might hold such a view. Do not be afraid to tackle the proposition. If you think that the statement is wrong or, more likely, flawed in some way, use your knowledge and understanding to deconstruct it. In answering this question, for example, you might end up demonstrating that whilst the first part of the quotation is less open to question, everything after the comma is arguable.

Approaching comparative questions

Most of the questions that you were asked in the AS examination were focused on a single country. Though you were given credit for illustrating your answers with relevant examples from other countries, the focus was clearly on one named country, namely the UK. For example, in an essay on electoral reform in the UK you might have been expected to mention the use of electoral systems in other countries, such as AMS in Germany or STV in the Republic of Ireland, perhaps even commenting on whether such systems have worked well in these countries. At A2, however, the questions are **explicitly** comparative. The comparative material provided in questions of this type does not just provide illustrations with which to highlight aspects of UK government and politics — it is designed to direct you towards the point of the question, encouraging you to compare the experience in two different countries. Examples of comparative questions are as follows:

- **Compare and contrast the roles and powers of the British prime minister with those of the US president.**
- **Do committees within the US Congress play a greater or lesser role than those within the UK Parliament?**
- **To what extent do senior members of the judiciary have a 'political' as well as a judicial role in the UK and the USA?**

Structure

Structure is the key to answering these explicitly comparative questions effectively. Two approaches are given below.

What similarities and differences exist between the constitutions of the USA and the UK?

Approach A

- introduce the topic by defining the term 'constitution'; make some comments about codified and uncodified constitutions
- move on to look at the US constitution and write two short paragraphs: one on origins and sources and one on principles and main elements
- look at the UK constitution and write two short paragraphs: one on origins and sources and one on principles and main elements
- reach a conclusion, comparing and contrasting the origins, sources and principles of the two constitutions

> **e** Though this approach has some merit (it is straightforward and allows you to reel off large chunks of pre-learnt material), it does not allow you to answer the question until the conclusion. However accurate the answer is in terms of factual content, it would be better to begin by identifying similarities and differences, and to sustain the comparison throughout. This would allow you to answer the question directly, and is a higher-level skill than simply telling the examiner everything you know.

Approach B

- provide an outline of the main areas of debate concerning constitutions; perhaps address the validity of terms such as codified/uncodified, flexible/rigid
- write four paragraphs: the **first** identifies similarities and differences between the origins of the two constitutions; the **second** looks at similarities and differences between the sources of the two constitutions; the **third** considers similarities and differences between the principles of the two constitutions; and the **fourth** deals with main elements
- draw together the key similarities and differences already identified; offer a final assessment

> **e** This is likely to be a far better response because it enables you to identify similarities and differences from an early point in the essay. This type of structure also makes it far more difficult to drift into lengthy passages of description without addressing the question. It is likely to lead to a more focused, analytical response.

Revision strategies

Four steps to success

Step 1

Your first task is to obtain a copy of the subject specification for the board you are studying, along with any past papers and other guidance that you can lay your hands on.

You also need to work out a realistic revision timetable. This should incorporate all of your subjects and be broken down into sessions of around 45 minutes divided by breaks. These breaks are important. If you leave no time for relaxation, you will be less likely to keep to the timetable and your revision will be less effective.

Step 2

Using the module content summaries from your specification, go through your folder and divide your notes into the various modules that you have studied. It might help you to photocopy the pages in the specification that summarise the content for each module and then put the relevant summaries on the top of each pile of notes.

Step 3

The next task is to check your notes in order to make sure that you have covered all of the elements in the specification. Are there big gaps? It may be that you have mislaid some notes, or that you missed some lessons and failed to catch up. It is also possible that your teacher has left out certain sections with good reason, and you should check this to make sure that you are not missing something vital. If you find that there are gaps that need filling, you need to work quickly. If the exam is still some way off, you may have time to reinforce any particularly thin topics by copying up notes from friends or undertaking some background reading of your own. If the problem is largely down to a lack of understanding — rather than a lack of notes — ask your teacher for help.

If the examination is only a few weeks away, however, you probably need a more drastic course of action. A number of books provide good factual summaries that may help you to cut corners if time is short: Anthony J. Bennett's *A2 US Government and Politics Exam Revision Notes* (Philip Allan Updates) or *AS & A-Level Government and Politics through Diagrams* (Oxford University Press) by Paul Fairclough, for example, allow you to get at the basics quickly.

Step 4

Look at the specification content and the past examination papers for each module. Which questions do you feel fairly confident about tackling? Which make you want to cry or retreat to your bed with a packet of custard creams? However tempting it is to start your revision with the topics you feel happy with, it really is better to grasp the nettle and address your weaknesses first. Once you have identified these weaker areas, you need to go through making summary notes. Try to get each small topic on to a single page. This process of summarising should produce a much less daunting set of revision notes. You could also try presenting your notes in different formats. Some books, for example, present the information in the form of diagrams. You could try turning these diagrams, and your own handwritten notes, into prose or into bullet-pointed lists. You will find that the process of reformatting your notes in this way reinforces learning and develops a greater understanding of the material.

Four strategies to avoid

(1) Staying at home when you should be attending in-school revision sessions. Though you may feel that you can do a better job yourself, the vast majority of students who adopt this approach do not achieve their potential. However pointless the school revision lessons may seem to you, they are probably helping you more than you realise.

(2) Revising for hours without a break or working for whole days on a single subject. A series of 45-minute sessions followed by 15-minute breaks can lead to more productive work and it is good to build some variety into your daily revision programme by mixing and matching different subjects.

(3) 'Question spotting'. Although it is good to look at the kinds of question that have been asked in the past, question spotting (i.e. trying to guess what the examiners will put on the exam paper) is a dangerous game. Even if your favourite topic does turn up, there is no guarantee that it is going to be phrased in such a way that you want to tackle it.

(4) Leaving out major topics. Ignoring major topics when you revise can be disastrous. Sometimes intelligent candidates score 35 marks out of 40 for one question, only to get 12 marks out of 40 for the second question because they have not revised the topic. Leaving out key topics is a particularly dangerous strategy for AQA Modules 4 and 5, for which Question 1 is compulsory and can be based on any part of the module content.

US Government & Politics

Questions and Answers

This section of the guide covers a range of answers to the kind of examination questions that you will be faced with at the end of your A2 course. It is divided into eight topics — Topics 1–4 deal with US government and Topics 5–8 cover US politics.

Each question has an indication of the amount of time that you might have in which to complete your answer. This is a guideline only — you should adjust these to the demands of the examination questions for your specification. The answers given here are not supposed to be perfect — each answer simply represents one way of approaching the question given and the grade that it might have achieved.

Examiner's comments

Examiner's comments are preceded by the icon **e**. Immediately after each question, before the student answer, there is an examiner's advice section which outlines the focus and scope of the question. Following each answer, an examiner's comment (in bold) summarises the main strengths and weaknesses of the answer. Shorter examiner's comments are inserted throughout the answers too. Read all of these examiner's advice and comment sections carefully — they indicate what you need to do in order to get an A-grade mark for the question.

The US constitution

Question 1.1

'The US constitution is entrenched and rigid. As a result, it presents a considerable barrier to political change.' To what extent is this view valid?

(45 minutes)

e The focus of this question is clearly the extent to which the US constitution makes political change in the USA difficult. The question also requires you to understand the meaning of terms such as 'entrenched' and 'rigid' in relation to a study of constitutions. Your first task is to explain what we mean when we say that 'the US constitution is entrenched and rigid'. It would be valid here to draw a brief comparison with the situation in the UK — but don't get carried away. Once you have done that, you should identify what you understand by the term 'political change' (e.g. constitutional change, ordinary legislative changes). You can then deal with the extent to which the entrenched nature of the US constitution does, indeed, present a barrier to each type of change.

▪ ▪ ▪

A-grade answer to question 1.1

The US constitution is often said to be 'entrenched and rigid', as the title states, because it is codified as a single, authoritative document. This is in contrast to the UK constitution which is uncodified and, therefore, often said to be more flexible than its US counterpart. Though this is the widely accepted view, the US constitution has in fact proven remarkably flexible and adaptable in the 200 years since it was written. Although it has been a barrier to political change, it has not prevented important and essential changes from taking place. We should also remember that many 'political changes' take place within the guidelines set out by the constitution.

e This is a focused and purposeful introduction. The candidate identifies the key words and challenges the assumptions in the title. However, an opportunity is missed to set out a clearer agenda, and give some idea of where the answer is going.

In the UK, parliament is said to be sovereign, but in the USA the constitution is sovereign. This means that the US government has to work within the constitution and any laws that contradict it are likely to be declared unconstitutional if they are brought before the US Supreme Court. This is because the court has had the power of judicial review since the *Marbury* v. *Madison* case in 1803. This means that the court can declare the actions of other branches of government (at state or federal government level) unconstitutional. This power can, of course, 'present a considerable barrier to political change', particularly those changes that bring one branch of government into conflict with another or bring government as a whole into conflict with the people.

> ℮ A sophisticated point is made here about sovereignty. The candidate clearly understands the way in which the constitution, through the Supreme Court, can provide a barrier to change.

Where the political change desired is in conflict with the constitution, the constitution will clearly provide a significant barrier. This is necessary. The Founding Fathers were keen to avoid a situation where the political system could be changed on the whim of the government of the day. The normal way of amending the constitution (two-thirds in House and Senate followed by three-quarters of state legislatures) ensures that only those changes that have overwhelming support across the USA are able to succeed. This is why there have only been 17 amendments since the Bill of Rights was agreed in 1791 and why an amendment as simple as the Equal Rights Amendment failed.

> ℮ The candidate exhibits sound knowledge (AO1) of the amendment process.

The only way to get around the need for an amendment in such cases is to hope that the US Supreme Court will interpret the existing constitution in such a way as to allow the desired political change. Even though the court can present a barrier to political change by interpreting the constitution in such a way as to strike down a law, it can also effect political change by interpreting the constitution more creatively. In 1954, for example, the court set the scene for desegregation in *Brown v. Board of Education, Topeka* where only 58 years earlier in *Plessy v. Fergusson*, 1896 they had interpreted the same passage in the constitution to allow segregation on trains. This example shows that though the amendment process is tortuous, changes in judicial interpretations can be just as effective in bringing about major political changes. Another good example is the New Deal. Even though the US Supreme Court said that some of the New Deal was unconstitutional, pressure from the public, Congress and the president (F. D. Roosevelt threatened to 'pack' the court) meant that one justice changed his position and the policies went through. This shows us that even things that are clearly unconstitutional can happen when the other branches of government let them go. This has also been seen with the limitations on personal freedoms since 11 September 2001.

Smaller, less controversial political change can be achieved by simply passing bills through Congress. However, even this is far from easy in the USA. The relative weakness of political parties, the separation of executive and legislature and the presence of 'divided government' at times lead to a situation in which the vast majority of bills fall at an early stage.

In conclusion, though the constitution does present a barrier to some major political changes, it is normally possible to get around this barrier if these changes are really needed. Many smaller political changes take place without the need for such tactics because they occur within the rules set out in the constitution.

e This is an excellent response, clearly worthy of a grade A. The candidate demonstrates a high level of knowledge and understanding, yet at the same time writes in an analytical rather than a descriptive manner. The discussion could perhaps have been structured a little more clearly from the outset, but this is still a very strong answer.

■ ■ ■

D-grade answer to question 1.1

The US constitution was written in 1787 by the Founding Fathers. The 55 delegates who went to the Philadelphia convention started off with the aim of reforming the Articles of the Confederation that had been in place since 1781 (following the War of Independence) but they decided to throw the articles away and start again from scratch, writing a new constitution.

Most of the delegates at the convention were keen to create a government that was fairer than that which they had experienced under the English before independence. They had read lots of books by people such as Locke, Paine and Montesquieu and wanted to create a limited government that had a separation of powers between executive, legislature and judiciary.

e Some good knowledge is demonstrated here, but this answer is already drifting away from analysis towards simple description. A descriptive approach is unlikely to achieve a good mark, however well it is carried out.

They spent most of their time debating how power should be divided between different parts of the government and how the needs of small states and large states should be balanced in the government. They didn't include a proper bill of rights in the original constitution but one was added by the passing of the first ten amendments in around 1791.

Since these amendments were agreed, there have only been another 17. This is because the Founding Fathers made the constitution very difficult to change. The main way of changing the constitution is to get two-thirds of the House and two-thirds of the Senate to propose an amendment and then three-quarters of states to agree to it. This is nearly impossible because even if you could get Congress to agree, there is virtually no chance of convincing three in four states. I think this is what the question means when it says that the constitution is entrenched and rigid.

Because most of the words of the constitution have stayed the same for over 200 years, it is often out of date so there are lots of arguments about what is allowed and what is not. The constitution says nothing about abortion, for example, so the Supreme Court has had to decide the rights and wrongs by interpreting it. This is called judicial activism. In this way, the constitution is not really a barrier to change because its meaning can be changed even if the actual words stay the same. This happened in 1954 with *Brown* v. *Board of Education, Topeka* saying that segregation was illegal. Before (in 1896

I think) they said that it was OK. So in that case there had been political change without the words of the constitution being changed at all.

 Although the quality of language is rather weak, this is a much stronger, more analytical paragraph. The knowledge is still evident, but here it is applied with more purpose. However, it would have been helpful to look at what judicial review is before leaping into judicial activism.

In conclusion, I don't think that the quote in the title is right because if political change is really needed then it can happen with a constitutional amendment or in the Supreme Court.

 This answer is rather short and overly descriptive. The penultimate paragraph gives us an idea of what the candidate is capable of doing, but this is not enough to lift the answer above a grade D.

■ ■ ■

Question 1.2

'Although the US system of government is said to be based on the doctrine of the separation of powers, the reality of the situation is far different.' Discuss.

(45 minutes)

 The key to answering this question is having a good appreciation of what is meant by the term 'separation of powers'. It is important to define this term early on in the essay, possibly explaining where the doctrine came from and its theoretical basis, i.e. that the three aspects of state power (executive, legislative and judicial) needed to be separated in order to prevent tyranny. Some understanding of the US context, i.e. why the Founding Fathers were attracted to this doctrine, would add something to your answer. You could then look at the way in which the doctrine is applied in the USA, both in law (i.e. the ways in which the US constitution separates power and people between the three branches of the federal government) and in practice (i.e. whether or not this separation actually works).

■ ■ ■

A-grade answer to question 1.2

When the Founding Fathers gathered to frame the US constitution in 1787 they had in common a fear of over-powerful government. Though they accepted that the Articles of Confederation that followed independence created too weak a government, they could still remember the oppressive style of government that they had experienced under the British. For many, the oppressive style of British rule was a direct

consequence of the fact that the powers of the legislature, the executive and the judiciary were not properly separated. The Founding Fathers were familiar with the work of men such as the French writer Montesquieu. He had put forward the idea of a separation of powers and highlighted the likelihood of tyrannical government if it was not in place. In Britain, the incomplete separation or partial fusion of powers had allowed the executive to exert too much control over the system. The Founding Fathers therefore sought to include in their new constitution a full separation of powers, thus setting the three branches up independently of one another and so being more able to hold each other back.

> **e** This is an excellent paragraph. The candidate provides a useful and accurate summary of the situation in the USA at the time that the constitution was written and, at the same time, defines key terms effectively.

The new constitution identified this separation of powers clearly: Article 1 begins 'all Legislative powers...shall be vested in a Congress of the United States'; Article 2 vests executive power in the president; and Article 3 places judicial power in the hands of the Supreme Court. Moreover, the membership of each branch of government was made separate. As a result, it is not possible for the president or other members of the executive to be members of the legislature. The president's cabinet members, for example, cannot be Congressmen in the same way that UK cabinet members are members of the Commons or the Lords. This separation of personnel should, therefore, make it less likely that one branch will roll over in favour of another.

> **e** The candidate makes a good point regarding the separation of personnel. Many candidates would simply focus on the separation of actual power, but this separation of individuals is crucial. Without it, the separation of powers would be fatally flawed.

In order to avoid the dangers of branches cooperating too much or simply capitulating, the Founding Fathers also staggered the length of terms of office for the various institutions. The Senate's term is 6 years with one-third elected every 2 years; the House of Representatives sits for 2 years; the president is elected every 4 years; and the Supreme Court sits for life. Staggering elections makes it more likely that different branches of government will be controlled by different political parties or different ideological coalitions, making it less likely that any coalition of interests can ever gain control of the whole. This control of different institutions by different parties or, in the case of the Supreme Court, supposedly neutral individuals (a phenomenon referred to as 'divided government') reinforces the desire of the various branches of government to check one another effectively.

This separation of powers was central to the constitution framed at Philadelphia, but a total separation of the powers to make laws, execute laws and enforce laws might have left government permanently gridlocked and unworkable. As a result, interconnections — 'checks and balances' — were built into the system of government. These provided enough linkage for the government to be effective while at the same time providing barriers against any one branch dominating the political process. Those in each branch know that they can achieve little alone but also know that they can, by negotiation, go some way towards achieving their goals. As Congressman Lee Hamilton acknowledged: 'The constitution only works when branches of government trust one another and cooperate.'

In domestic policy, for example, there is significant overlap between the powers afforded to the various branches. Though Congress (holding legislative power) has the right to make laws, the president (as head of the executive) is charged with the task of ensuring that these laws are 'faithfully executed'. The president's right to 'speak to Congress from time to time regarding the state of the Union' has become something of an agenda-setting exercise in which the president sets out the measures that he or she would like to see legislated for in the State of the Union Address. The president's right to veto legislation also gives the ultimate power to prevent those measures that he or she disapproves of passing into law.

In the area of foreign policy, the situation is also complex. The president is given the role of commander-in-chief of the armed forces, yet it is only Congress that has the power to formally declare war. The president can also act as the 'chief diplomat' and negotiate treaties on behalf of the United States, but such treaties require the approval of two-thirds of the Senate to be ratified.

These are only brief illustrations. It can be said, however, that a total separation of powers does not exist in the US constitution. Moreover, such a total separation would prove unworkable because there needs to be a degree of linkage and coordination between the three branches in order for anything to be achieved. Thus the system of separation of powers enshrined in the US constitution is less of a total separation — that might work well as a theory but be difficult or counterproductive to enforce — and more of a system of divided and shared powers, allowing cooperation at a distance while avoiding the kind of concentration of power that might result in the sort of tyranny that writers such as Montesquieu feared.

How well then does this system of shared powers work in practice? For every commentator who feels that Congress and the Supreme Court fail to provide an effective check on the unconstitutional expansion of presidential power, there is another who criticises the way in which the US political system is prone to inaction and gridlock due to the fragmentation of power.

When in 1973 Arthur Schlesinger wrote of *The Imperial Presidency*, for example, he highlighted the massive expansion that had taken place in presidential power since the start of the twentieth century, particularly in the field of foreign affairs. 'The constitution', as Schlesinger noted, 'has never greatly bothered any wartime president.' In contrast, President Gerald Ford, only 2 years after Schlesinger's comments, felt moved to describe the presidency as 'impaired' or even 'imperilled', and Francis Biddle concluded that 'the separate powers are now too separate' with Washington divided by a series of 'bunkers' held by 'mutually suspicious troops'.

Clearly, then, the key to the application of the separation of powers and the workings of the associated checks and balances lies in flexibility. An impartial observer can at one moment note an excessive concentration of power in the hands of the president only to later see a system where the fragmentation of power leads to gridlock and inaction — this is testament to the way in which the interconnections between the various branches of government bend and adapt to the needs of each age.

The ability to write a lot in timed conditions is an advantage and this answer is very long. More important than how much you write, however, is the quality of what you write. This answer is analytical throughout. Every point is illustrated with appropriate examples. Every idea is communicated with clarity and with a full subject-specific vocabulary. This is an A-grade answer and would probably achieve full marks.

■ ■ ■

C/B-grade answer to question 1.2

The separation of powers is a main principle of the US constitution. The Founding Fathers split power up between three branches of government — legislature, executive and judiciary. They did this to make sure that the executive couldn't dominate things the way that it did in Britain. Over here, the executive is dominated by the leader of the majority party in the Commons and this means that the prime minister can normally get any laws through. When Thatcher's government introduced the poll tax in the late 1980s she had a massive Conservative majority in the Commons and was able to push it through parliament, even though it was not a very good piece of legislation.

The candidate provides a fairly clear definition and a relevant example. It is important not to become carried away with the UK content when writing an essay on a US politics paper.

In America the president is totally separate from Congress. He or she is elected separately, unlike the PM in the UK, and is not allowed to be part of Congress — again, unlike the PM. This is not just true of the president. No one in the executive can be a member of the legislative branch and no one in the executive or the legislative branches can be part of the judiciary. Again, this is different from in Britain. Over here the Lord Chancellor is part of the executive, a member of the legislature (in the Lords) and the top of the judiciary. Some writers in the eighteenth century believed that this overlap could lead to a kind of dictatorship.

In the USA the Congress has the legislative powers. This means that it has the role of making laws. The president has the executive powers and has the job of executing laws. The Supreme Court holds the top judicial power and is there to judge people against the laws. Because the constitution is 'sovereign' the court can also declare things unconstitutional if they break the rules set out by the Founding Fathers. Although these powers appear separate, however, the various parts of government are linked together by checks and balances. This means that the three branches really share powers and monitor each other.

The president has a number of checks on Congress. He effectively recommends/ proposes legislation through the State of the Union Address. He can veto legislation and he can call special sessions of Congress. The president also has checks on the Supreme Court. He can appoint top federal judges including Supreme Court justices. He can also issue pardons, thus reversing judicial action.

Congress has a number of checks on the president. It can reject, amend or delay the president's legislative proposals. The president's budget also has to be approved by Congress. Congress can override the president's veto (with a two-thirds majority in each house) and many presidential appointments have to be approved by a majority vote in the Senate. Congress has a lot of influence on foreign policy too. A two-thirds majority is required in the Senate for treaties to be ratified and Congress retains the War Power. In theory, it can even prevent the president entering a war or force him into one against his or her will. Ultimately, Congress can initiate impeachment proceedings against presidents as it did in the case of Bill Clinton. Congress also exerts power over the Supreme Court. Congress (the Senate) confirms Supreme Court appointments by majority vote and controls the size and jurisdiction of the court. Congress can also start constitutional amendments which change the constitution if it doesn't like the way in which the court is interpreting the words that are there already.

The Supreme Court has checks on the president and on Congress. Through judicial review the Supreme Court can declare the actions of the president and Congress unconstitutional, thus making them void. The court can also interpret the meaning of acts, affecting the way in which they are implemented.

e These paragraphs on checks and balances are accurate but they tend towards the descriptive rather than the analytical. The content should be made part of the argument — it seems here as though the candidate has simply inserted a pre-learnt descriptive section in the middle of the essay.

So although there is a separation of powers in the US system, the powers are actually shared between the different branches through these checks and balances.

e **This is a reasonable response given the time available. There is enough here to suggest that the candidate could probably have written a far more convincing response, but this answer is limited because it leans towards the descriptive rather than the analytical.**

Congress

O&A

Question 2.1

'Though greater power rests with the House of Representatives, the Senate holds greater prestige.' Assess the validity of this statement.

(45 minutes)

🅔 Take great care when answering questions of this type. The temptation is to take the proposition at face value, and simply put together an answer that supports the statement. The question, however, asks you to 'assess the validity of this statement', not simply to back it up. If you keep this at the forefront of your mind, it should not be too difficult a question to answer. As long as you have a good knowledge of the power and status of each chamber, you should be able to come to a reasoned judgement. Avoid spending the first half of your essay on the House and the second half on the Senate. Instead, try to identify areas or paragraph themes (e.g. 'domestic policy', 'composition', 'scrutiny') and then look at the House and Senate within each themed paragraph, focusing throughout on power and prestige.

■ ■ ■

A-grade answer to question 2.1

The two chambers of Congress, House and Senate, hold equal legislative power but they are in many respects very different places. Some commentators see this as a result of their different compositions. Others point to the fact that the House and the Senate are also given other roles by the constitution and that these roles give each chamber its distinctive character.

The title advances two clear propositions first that the House 'holds more power' and second that the Senate 'holds more prestige', and it is worthwhile examining each proposition in turn. The first proposition is, at best, questionable. The power over legislation is divided equally between the House and the Senate. Either chamber can bring about the end of a given piece of legislation and versions of bills normally start their passage through Congress in both chambers at the same time. There is no assumption that the House has the final say, as is the case with the Commons in the UK, because the Senate (unlike the Lords) is elected and therefore has as much right to pass judgement on the merits of a bill as the House. There is no US equivalent to the Parliament Act in the UK. The only respect in which the House can be considered privileged is the way in which it has the right to hear all money bills first. This is a legacy of a time when the House was the only elected chamber (i.e. before the 17th Amendment). The only other significant powers held exclusively by the House are the power to impeach any member of the federal government, executive or judicial branches and to choose a president in the event that no candidate has received a majority in the Electoral College. It is therefore hard to see why the House might be considered a more powerful chamber. Indeed, the Senate could reasonably claim to be more powerful than the House, as we will see.

> These two opening paragraphs are promising. The candidate focuses on the question from the outset and has an analytical style that combines argument and supporting material fluently and with a degree of clarity.

The Senate, unlike the House, has a range of powers that are exclusive to it, as opposed to being held jointly. In the area of foreign policy in particular, the Senate has a significant role. All treaties negotiated by the president are subject to ratification by two-thirds of the Senate. This is not a theoretical power. The Senate has rejected a number of important treaties, including Versailles in 1919 and Carter's SALT II Treaty in the 1970s. In addition to this power the Senate also has the role of confirming presidential appointments (by simple majority). This power extends from appointments to the Supreme Court to the appointment of foreign ambassadors. Again, this power has been used on a number of occasions — for example, when Senators rejected Reagan's nomination of Robert Bork for the US Supreme Court. The Senate also has the role of trying cases of impeachment where the House has brought the case (a two-thirds majority is needed for conviction) and of electing a vice president, where two or more candidates are tied. Perhaps, then, the Senate actually has more power than the House.

To a certain extent, the nature and range of the Senate's powers contribute to its greater prestige. Its role in foreign policy, in particular, may give the impression that the Senate's members are more statesmanlike. There are, however, a number of other factors that might make the chamber and/or its members appear more prestigious.

> This is a very effective 'linking paragraph'. Through this link, the essay is able to move smoothly from a discussion of power to a discussion of prestige.

First, there is the issue of composition. The Senate is considerably smaller (100 members) than the House (435 members). This means that the Senate is seen as being rather more exclusive than the House. The smaller size of the chamber also allows for a different style of debate. In the Senate there is the time and the space for individual Senators to speak at length (consider filibusters) and to deal with a lot of Senate business in the Chamber itself rather than sending it all down to committees, as happens in the House. The Senatorial term of office is 6 years (only 2 in the House). This also makes the Senate appear a little less frenetic. In the House, members always have to think about re-election (the 'permanent campaign') whereas Senators have the ability to establish themselves and even to do things that might be unpopular in the short term.

The fact that candidates for the Senate must be 30 years old or over (only 25 years in the House) means that a place in the Senate is often seen as something that politicians aspire to later in their careers, having gained a degree of experience and maturity in other positions. Indeed, many House members eventually seek election in the Senate, whereas far fewer would consider moving in the other direction. This is surely a reflection of the relative prestige of the two chambers. A significant minority of those in the Senate (perhaps 40%) are millionaires and this would also suggest that the 100 positions available in the Senate carry great prestige and are in demand.

Clearly, then, whereas the first proposition in the title (that the House is more powerful) is questionable, there are a number of very good reasons why the second (that the Senate carries more prestige) is true — most of these relate to its size, composition and terms of office.

It is difficult to find fault with this answer. The candidate writes with great purpose and fluency. From the outset, there is a clear idea of where the discussion is going and the use of linking sentences allows the discussion to move smoothly from point to point. This is a top A-grade response.

C/D-grade answer to question 2.1

The US constitution vests all legislative power in the US Congress. This Congress consists of the House of Representatives and the US Senate. The House and the Senate share a number of roles and at the same time have a number of roles that they hold exclusively as a chamber. Congress as a whole holds the power to: pass laws; pass the budget; undertake investigations into the actions of the executive branch; start constitutional amendments by a two-thirds majority in each House; declare war; and confirm the appointment of a newly-elected vice president.

This material is accurate but it does not really constitute an introduction. An effective introduction would outline the scope of the answer and address one or more of the key words included in the title. This is simply a summary of Article 1 of the constitution. The impression is that the candidate would have written this as an introduction to any question on Congress, regardless of the subtleties of the question set.

The House of Representatives has 435 members, divided between the 50 US states on the basis of population. Alaska has one Representative, whereas California has 53. The term of office is 2 years and the whole House is re-elected every 2 years. Candidates must be 25 years old or over, a citizen of the USA for more than 7 years and resident in the state for which they are standing. Of House members, 14% are women, 13% are black or Hispanic and 36% are lawyers. The House holds a number of exclusive powers. It has, for example, the right to consider all money bills first. This power was originally given to the House because it was the only directly elected chamber (until the 17th

Amendment, 1913). The House also has the power to impeach any member of the federal government, executive or judicial branches and to choose a president in the event that no candidate has received a majority in the Electoral College.

The US Senate consists of 100 members, two for each of the 50 states regardless of the size of states. This was part of the Connecticut compromise between smaller and larger states. The term of office is 6 years and one-third of the Senate is elected every 2 years. Candidates must be 30 years old or over, a citizen of the USA for 9 or more years and a resident in the state for which they are standing. Of the Senators, 13 are women, none are black or Hispanic and 53 are lawyers. As is the case with the House, the Senate holds a number of powers exclusively. All presidential treaties must be ratified by a two-thirds majority in the Senate before they can become law. The Senate also gets to decide whether or not to confirm many federal appointments (e.g. Supreme Court justices) by simple majority. When the House brings an impeachment case, the Senate has the power to try cases of impeachment (a two-thirds majority is needed for conviction). Where two or more candidates are tied, the Senate also has the power to elect a vice president.

Again, lots more factual description is provided. The candidate shows excellent knowledge (AO1) but there is no real analysis, evaluation, focus or direction (AO2 and AO3).

In addition to having very different compositions and some exclusive powers, the two chambers are different in terms of style. Because the House has 435 members, it is more difficult to have proper debates and, as a result, most of its real work is done in numerous committees and sub-committees. In the Senate, however, there are only 100 members. The Senate tends, therefore, to be more of a proper debating chamber and there is even a tradition that members can speak for as long as they like (this is called a filibuster), whereas in the House members are normally limited to around 5 minutes. Between one-third and one-half of Senators are said to be millionaires and this is another reason why they might have more prestige.

This is a very descriptive answer. The candidate makes little attempt, if any, to relate the discussion to the question and would be lucky to get a grade C, despite the good factual knowledge. A more focused and analytical intro-duction, setting out the direction and scope of the answer and acknowl-edging the subtleties of the question, would have resulted in a better answer.

Question 2.2

What factors determine the outcome of votes within Congress?

(30 minutes)

e This type of question gives you the opportunity to hit the ground running. The key to writing a good answer is to identify a number of 'factors' — between three and five — and to deal with the importance of each factor in its own paragraph. Try to deal with your factors in a logical order, if there is an obvious one, and remember to connect factors with linking phrases to give an impression of confidence and fluency.

A-grade answer to question 2.2

In Britain the party is everything. As Disraeli advised his colleagues in parliament, 'damn your principles, stick with your party'. In the USA, however, the situation is rather more complicated, not least because US political parties are far weaker than their UK counterparts.

e It would be better to provide a slightly more comprehensive introduction, one that sets out a clearer agenda for the discussion ahead. That said, this is certainly focused and sets up part of the debate.

Those comparing the influence of US party 'whips' and their namesakes in the UK have often concluded that in the USA the whips have no 'sting'. This is partly because of the fact that parties cannot threaten to deselect candidates (because constituents have control of this through congressional primaries) and they cannot offer promotion to the executive, due to the separation of powers. If we take a 'party vote' to be a vote where the majority of one party votes for a measure and the majority of the other party votes against, then only 43% of House and 49% of Senate votes were 'party votes' in 2000.

In order to appeal to the nation as a whole in presidential elections, parties also have to adopt a raft of policies that will offend as few people as possible. The resulting 'platform' is often extremely vague and allows individual congressional candidates to tailor elements to their own constituencies. The parties are, therefore, ideologically weak and decentralised compared to their counterparts in the UK — they are truly 'broad churches'.

If the party has little influence upon the voting behaviour of those in Congress, it could be argued that a Congressman's conscience (his or her 'principles') hold even less sway. Some members of Congress clearly have views on particular issues that sometimes do not allow them to follow the 'party line'. On the issue of abortion, for example, some Democrats are committed 'pro-lifers' even though their party has explicitly endorsed a 'pro-choice' position since the 1992 presidential election. That said, Democrats uneasy over abortion have increasingly been forced to 'toe the line'. Al Gore, Jesse Jackson and Representative Richard A. Gephardt, for example, have all, as the *New York Times* noted, 'jettisoned their previous reservations about abortion'. US Senators driven by a conscientious objection to a particular policy at least retain a potent weapon in the filibuster, even if it is rarely used to its limit.

Having dealt with the influence of 'party', the candidate moves on to deal with other possible influences. This shows that the response is structured well.

If party and conscience really have so little influence over votes within Congress, what factors might determine the outcome of votes? Members of Congress, it is argued, are under so much pressure from their constituents that they cannot maintain as slavish an obedience to the party line as MPs generally do in the UK. Members of Congress have to take a good deal more notice of their constituents than most MPs in the UK. This is partly because it is constituents who select candidates through congressional primaries and partly because representatives in the House face election every 2 years, as do one-third of Senators. Though the vast majority of those Members of Congress who seek re-election are successful (98% of those House members and 82.8% for the Senate), they are able to achieve this success, at least in part, by carefully cultivating links with their constituents. They also have to try to 'bring home the bacon' for their constituents by securing valuable contracts ('pork') for their states.

The executive, in the form of the president, can have significant influence over individual members of Congress. First, the president can use his or her friends. The vice president, party leaders in Congress and the chief of staff can all put the case. Second, the president can use personal persuasion, for example, by making telephone calls, by entertaining or by offering 'pork' or help in the election campaign. House members, facing re-election every 2 years, are particularly receptive to this kind of persuasion.

The pressures of re-election also create a need for campaign finance and this creates an opening for pressure groups. By forming Political Action Committees (PACs), pressure groups can maximise their financial contributions to candidates' campaigns, bypassing the 1974 Campaign Finance Act. During the 1980s groups such as Jerry Falwell's Moral Majority undertook a series of campaigns not only to raise public awareness, but also to back sympathetic candidates and attack unsympathetic ones. They claimed to have registered 10 million votes for Ronald Reagan and attacked liberal Senators including Birch Bayle, George McGovern and Frank Church for their positions on issues such as abortion.

Clearly, then, there are a number of factors that influence the voting behaviour of Congressmen. The diversity and scale of the USA has limited the extent to which political parties can provide real control over those members who achieve elected office. The American system favours pressure group activity and makes Congressmen focus on the constituents.

This answer could have begun more impressively. The introduction, though adequate, could outline the scope of the answer more explicitly. Having said that, the candidate has produced an answer that is structured well and is analytical throughout. It would achieve a grade A.

C-grade answer to question 2.2

The main factor that determines how Congressmen act in Congress and, therefore, the outcome of congressional votes is the needs of the Congressman's state or district. This is especially true for those in the House of Representatives. House members have to be re-elected every 2 years and they have to be selected to represent their party through primaries before the main election even takes place. This means that they always have to think about re-election and so they really have to listen to what their constituents think. If they ignore their constituents, then they won't even be selected as a candidate, let alone be re-elected.

> The candidate clearly understands the question and identifies one factor in this introductory paragraph. The danger is that the essay might focus entirely on this factor, leaving it lacking in range and balance.

As a result of this, Congressmen try to do as much as they can to make their voters happy. This might mean making speeches in Congress raising issues that concern their constituents. People keep a close eye on what their representatives are doing in Washington and Congressmen work hard to get their names into the *Congressional Record* (a little like *Hansard* in the UK). Some pressure groups even publish detailed records of how Congressmen are voting on certain issues relevant to the voters in their home state. This means that House members and Senators have to be careful about how they vote on particular issues.

Congressmen also try to get real benefits for their constituents by 'log-rolling'. This is where Congressmen work together to make amendments to pieces of legislation that are passing through the legislature. These amendments, called 'riders', bring benefits to their districts or states and may have nothing to do with the original piece of legislation at all. Congressmen also try to get benefits for their constituents by doing deals with the president. The president sometimes uses the promise of federal contracts to persuade key members of Congress to support his policies. Committee chairs, majority/minority leaders and elder statesmen in both chambers are targets for this kind of treatment.

Other factors may be important too. The position of Congress members' parties or their conscience may influence how they vote on particular issues, but the main concern has to be getting re-elected (especially in the House) and this overrules everything else. This is shown where southern Republican Congressmen often side with southern Democrats rather than northerners from their own party. Parties have more differences within them than between them.

> **This is a shorter answer than the previous one, but that need not necessarily be a problem. The main flaw is not its length, but the fact that the candidate only really deals effectively with one factor that influences voting in Congress. In the last paragraph there is a somewhat belated attempt to put this one factor into context alongside others, but this is too little too late. The**

candidate clearly has the ability to achieve a higher grade, but would only achieve a strong grade C.

■ ■ ■

Question 2.3

Assess the role and importance of committees within the US Congress.

(45 minutes)

 In order to do this question justice you need to have a good overall understanding of the way in which Congress works. Without this it is difficult to put the work of congressional committees into context. That said, a sound knowledge of the range, roles, powers and importance of the committees that operate within Congress is required too. One way into the essay might be to demonstrate an understanding of the sheer volume and complexity of work facing the House and the Senate. Doing this will help show why committees are likely to be so important. Remember that although the House of Representatives is often referred to as 'Congress' in the USA, Congress is — strictly speaking — both the House and the Senate. Your discussion should, therefore, include both chambers.

■ ■ ■

A-grade answer to question 2.3

Boris Marshalov, a Russian visitor to the US Congress, remarked: 'Congress is so strange. A man gets up to speak and says nothing. Nobody listens — and then everybody disagrees.' What he was referring to is the way in which the House of Representatives meeting as a chamber is simply an opportunity for members to make a few points on behalf of their state rather than a real debating chamber. Marshalov might have better understood what he was witnessing if he had had the benefit of Woodrow Wilson's insight. Wilson remarked: 'Congress in session is Congress on show, Congress in committee is Congress at work.'

 It can often be difficult to use quotations effectively. Ideally, they should be short, punchy and used only to support or introduce an element of your argument, rather than to replace it. Although you would not normally use two full quotations in a single paragraph, this candidate gets away with it because of the quality of the quotations themselves and the way in which they have been integrated so seamlessly into the introduction.

It would be difficult — if not impossible — for the House of Representatives to deal with even a quarter of its workload on the floor of the House itself. The chamber only consists of 435 members, yet must legislate to govern a nation of 290 million people

that is the largest economy in the world. The solution to this conundrum is, as Wilson recognised, that most of the work is delegated to the 17 permanent standing committees in the House and over 200 subcommittees that work under them. In the UK, permanent departmental select committees scrutinise the work of departments, whereas legislation is dealt with by more ad hoc standing committees. In the USA however, the House's 17 permanent standing committees are full-time legislative powerhouses, able to make and break any piece of legislation that comes before them.

e This is a well-written and fairly accurate paragraph outlining the reasons why congressional committees are so central to the legislative process.

At the beginning of each session, each committee has a number of executive meetings to try to work out a possible order in which the committee will look at the bills presented to it. Committee chairmen play a key role in prioritising bills. Many bills are simply 'pigeonholed' (put to one side and effectively killed). Those bills that avoid 'pigeonholing' are then subject to hearings. Many members of Congress are trained lawyers (36% in the House, 56% in the Senate in 2001) and as a result the committee hearings are similar to trial in format, with evidence being brought forward by specialists and interested parties alike in the belief that, as Ernest S. Griffith observed, 'truth customarily emerges from a battle of protagonists'. In addition, members of the committees themselves often have a good deal of expertise in the work of their committee because they tend to retain their positions in these permanent committees for some time.

Pressure groups with an interest in a particular piece of legislation send professional lobbyists to the committee hearings and to meet the committee members they feel might be sympathetic to their case. Committees also spend a considerable amount of time, and money, conducting independent research. For example, 200 investigators were sent to Europe after the Second World War to check the Marshall Plan. Only after such hearings does the committee consider the fate of the bill and amend it (if necessary) in light of the evidence. This is called the marking-up session. It is then reported out of the committee back to the chamber. Committees can be forced to report out a bill that they have 'sat on', but this is rare.

The chairmen of standing committees and their subcommittees wield considerable power over the agenda and procedure of the committees and, as a result, committee chairmen can exert a great deal of influence in the House and the Senate. This is particularly true of those chairing major committees. In the past, committee chairs were filled largely on the basis of seniority — the member with the longest continuous period of service on the committee became its chair. In the 1960s this resulted in many of the top committee chairmen jobs being permanently occupied by a handful of old, white, southern Democrats. During the 1970s, however, the Democrats made some major changes to the committee system, including the effective abolition of the old seniority system (1971) and an agreement that if 20% of a committee's members so desired, the committee chair would be elected by the committee.

A number of key committees play a particularly important role in the passage of legislation. Of these the House Rules Committee is probably the most important. Riker described the House Rules Committee as: 'a toll bridge attendant who argues and bargains with each prospective customer: who lets his friends go free, who will not let his enemies pass at any price.' It is the first port of call for most bills once they have been reported out of committees ready for the second reading. The House Rules Committee assigns each bill a rule which stipulates the date on which it is to be heard and the degree of debate and amendment that it will be subject to. The committee can place a bill under one of three types of 'Rule': an open rule, which allows the bill to be amended without limits (i.e. 'to death'); a closed rule (which restricts the amendments which can be passed); and a special rule (which demands the House considers the bill immediately). Like other standing committees, the House Rules Committee has the power to pigeonhole a bill, but the House can force it to release a bill by passing a 'discharge petition' with a simple majority.

e This is an excellent section on the House Rules Committee. The content is impressive but, at the same time, is fundamentally analytical rather than descriptive.

The ultimate test of how important any element of the political system is should be the way in which other elements of the system view it. In the case of House standing committees, it is clear that everyone in Washington, including presidents past and present, recognises the importance of having key committees and, in particular, key committee chairmen 'on-side'. This is reflected in the extent to which presidents have been prepared to lavish 'pork' on these individuals. An example is the case of Mendel Rivers, who was Chairman of the Armed Services Committee 1965–70. During this time he gained 11 major new naval installations for his state (South Carolina), including shipyards, missile bases, hospitals and training camps. The Bureau of Naval Personnel and the Naval Reserve Headquarters were both moved to his state and he also had a complex of buildings named after him.

e **It is probably best to avoid bringing a lot of new material into your conclusion, but in this case the candidate manages it effectively. This is not an orthodox conclusion, but it refers back to the title and offers a reasoned judgement. Overall, this answer would achieve a solid grade A, though greater attention to Senate committees would have provided a more balanced answer.**

The presidency and the executive branch

Question 3.1

'The president is at liberty, both in law and in conscience, to be as big a man as he can' (Woodrow Wilson). How effective are the limitations on presidential power?

(45 minutes)

Many candidates welcome questions such as this, as it is a topic with which they are familiar. However, you must look carefully at the way in which the question is phrased before reeling off a pre-learnt 'power of the president' essay. This question requires you to consider the effectiveness of limitations on the president's powers, so you probably need to restructure or fine tune your learnt plan to this line of inquiry. The theory and factual information that you use will, therefore, be largely the same, but you need to come at it from a slightly different angle. It might be a good idea to drop the word 'limitation(s)' into your answer every now and then, just to show that you are answering this question.

A-grade answer to question 3.1

Some of the Founding Fathers wanted a strong president. 'Energy in the executive,' stated Alexander Hamilton, 'is a leading character in the definition of good government.' Others, however, were concerned that the president could become too powerful and become, effectively, a monarch — particularly in times of emergency. In the end, the constitution granted the president a number of powers in both domestic and foreign policy, whilst putting in place a series of checks and balances designed to control the president's powers.

So what powers does the modern president have in domestic and foreign policy, what limitations exist on these powers and how effective are these limitations?

This is an important sentence because it recognises that although this question might well deal with presidential powers, the emphasis is on the limitations on these powers rather than on the powers themselves.

The president's constitutional powers are fairly modest. In domestic policy he or she can make proposals through the State of the Union Address, sign or veto legislation, act as chief executive, nominate executive branch domestic policy officials and top judges and issue pardons. A number of constitutional checks limit the president's power in these areas. Though the president has the job of delivering the State of the Union Message, it is Congress that makes the laws in the first place. No member of the executive is allowed to be a member of the legislature (due to the separation of powers) and the president therefore has to rely on friends in Congress to pass the legislation that he or she wants. This is very different from the prime minister's situation in the UK. Whilst the US president can veto legislation passed by Congress, he must do so within 10 days and provide a written note explaining his reasons for doing so. Even then, Congress can overturn his veto if it can secure a two-thirds majority in each chamber. The president's power to veto is, therefore, limited by Congress's ability to override this veto. The president's executive appointments require Senate approval in most cases, too. For example, President Bush's nomination of John Tower as Secretary of Defense was rejected in 1989 and Reagan failed to get approval for his appointment of Robert Bork to the US Supreme Court.

In foreign policy, the president is given the role of commander-in-chief, with the power to negotiate treaties and appoint executive branch foreign policy staff and foreign ambassadors and envoys. Here too, though, presidential powers are limited, in theory at least. Though the president is commander-in-chief, it is Congress that holds the power to declare war. Though the president can negotiate treaties, they have to be ratified by the Senate (by a two-thirds majority). For example, Woodrow Wilson had the Versailles Treaty rejected and Carter failed to gain approval for his SALT II agreement with the Russians.

e Dividing the discussion into 'domestic' and 'foreign' policy provides a reasonable structure here, and the candidate gives a clear and accurate summary of the president's powers in each area along with the limitations acting upon them.

From this it might appear that the limitations on the power of the president are considerable. The reality is, however, a little different from the impression given by the constitution. Aaron Wildavsky (in his book *The Two Presidencies*) concluded that the USA has ended up with, in effect, two presidencies: a 'Domestic Policy President' and a 'Foreign Policy President'. Presidents who have been thwarted by Congress in their domestic programmes have succeeded repeatedly in persuading Congress to give in to them on foreign policy. This has happened for a number of reasons. First, the constitution divided domestic legislative powers between legislature and executive far more clearly than it divided foreign policy powers. Second, members of Congress are more likely to be concerned about domestic policy because their re-election is more dependent upon it. Third, successful modern foreign policy is, by its very nature, difficult to formulate in a Congress numbering 535 individuals.

e Wildavsky's 'two presidencies' thesis is something that only normally appears in the strongest candidates' answers. You would certainly not need to make this point in order to get a grade A, but demonstrating wider knowledge such as this creates a favourable impression and supports the candidate's argument.

Since the Founding Fathers wrote the constitution, however, the USA has changed dramatically, as has the world. Several factors have, therefore, led to an expansion in the role of the president. For example, Congressmen have been too willing to delegate unconstitutional powers to the president in times of crisis when public opinion is against them. They show a tendency to allow the president to make decisions that they themselves are not prepared to make. The Supreme Court has also failed to make decisions on critical areas (e.g. Vietnam) and been scared into submission in other areas (e.g. over the New Deal's Industrial Recovery Act and Agricultural Adjustment Act). The federal government has also expanded and the president's role as part of the government has therefore increased accordingly. The international role of the USA has increased massively since the time of the constitution and as a result the president has become the representative of the nation, rather than just one part of the tripartite government. This has been emphasised by the USA having superpower status — particularly since the collapse of the USSR — and by the rise of the mass media. The role of 'head of state' has, therefore, expanded.

As a result of these changes, the president is now not only chief executive, chief diplomat, and commander-in-chief but also chief legislator, chief war- and peacemaker, head of state and head of his party. In his book *The Imperial Presidency*, Arthur Schlesinger outlined what he saw as the massive increase in presidential power since the framing of the constitution, particularly in foreign policy.

The Founding Fathers knew that the president might need to use extraordinary power when faced with emergencies. It was partly for this reason that they left foreign policy powers deliberately vague and overlapping when framing the constitution. They wanted to provide the potential for speed of action and flexibility whilst at the same time avoiding some permanent grant of major military power into the hands of one man. Though the power to declare war was placed firmly and clearly in the hands of Congress, therefore, they knew that the president might need to take independent action and return to Congress later. Schlesinger charted the rise of 'presidential wars' — wars in all but name that were never formally declared by Congress but justified, most often, on the grounds of emergency or self-defence (such as in the case of Vietnam). The power to ratify treaties was given to the Senate, as we have seen already, but, faced with Senate opposition, presidents began to make treaties by other names. These so-called executive agreements had the same legal power as treaties (*US* v. *Pink*) but — because they were not called treaties — they bypassed the requirement for Senate ratification.

Thus we can see that whilst the president's powers are subject to checks and balances, presidents can often get around these barriers, particularly in emergencies, where the other branches of government step aside or where presidents side-step the wording of the constitution.

🄴 **This is an exceptionally strong answer. It is also very long. Despite its length, however, the candidate never loses touch with the question. Each argument is illustrated with good examples which don't get in the way of the answer** itself. **Overall, the answer is fluently written and excellent on both theory and practice.**

◼ ◼ ◼

D-grade answer to question 3.1

I agree with Woodrow Wilson that: 'the president is at liberty, both in law and in conscience, to be as big a man as he can.' This is because the office of the president is far more important now than it was when the constitution was written in 1787.

Although the constitution granted all legislative power to the Congress in Article I, the president is now the main legislator. Presidents cannot be a part of Congress, due to the separation of powers, but they make the State of the Union Address and this is now a little like the Queen's Speech in the UK in which the government is able to set out all of the policies that it intends to bring in. Presidents can normally get what they want by offering bribes ('pork') to important Congressmen or by being nice to them or offering them help with their campaigns. Presidents are so well known now that Congress is sometimes scared to stand up to them because they are so worried about being re-elected. The president can 'wrap himself in the flag' and use patriotism to bully Congress into passing policies. Congress hardly ever rejects presidential laws.

America is the last great superpower in the world and the US president is the army leader (commander-in-chief). This means that they can control the army and fight wars whenever they want to. Congress has the power to declare war but the president can normally find an excuse to fight wars without declaring them if he or she can make out that he or she is acting in an emergency, especially if it is to defend America (like Johnson said in Vietnam or Bush did in Iraq and Afghanistan). Really, it's all about presidents having the guts to 'go for it'. If they do have, then Congress is normally prepared to let them get away with it in foreign policy because most members of Congress are not voted in on foreign policy issues. Neither are presidents — as Bill Clinton said: 'it's the economy, stupid.'

So the president really is 'at liberty, both in law and in conscience, to be as big a man as he can'.

ℰ This candidate clearly knows something about the power of the presidency but fails to secure a good grade as a result of three key factors. First, this answer is far too brief. Although quality is better than quantity, more quantity than this is needed if you are to develop your arguments beyond the basic. Second, the candidate does not focus on the question explicitly enough. Third, the answer presented is one-sided. Whilst it is fine to make a judgement in the conclusion, you should avoid making one in your introduction and then only including information that backs it up in the essay that follows.

Question 3.2

Assess the importance of the roles of the vice president.

(15 minutes)

 You only have a relatively short amount of time in which to deal with this question. It is important, therefore, that you get into your stride quickly, outlining the roles of the vice president — with examples — and considering the importance of these roles individually and, at the end, collectively, by passing your judgement on the office.

■ ■ ■

A-grade answer to question 3.2

The vice president has a number of key constitutional roles. First, he acts as the president of the Senate, having the right to chair debates and cast the deciding vote when the Senate is tied. Dick Cheney, for example, cast such a deciding vote in April 2001 in support of George W. Bush's tax-cutting measures. Second, the vice president has the responsibility of becoming president in the event of the president's incapacity, death, resignation or impeachment. For example, Johnson took over from Kennedy following the latter's assassination, Ford took over from Nixon following Nixon's resignation and George Bush Senior took over from Reagan temporarily following the attempt on Reagan's life in 1985. As James Baker noted, the vice president is only 'a heartbeat away from the big office'.

Despite the fact that 13 former vice presidents have gone on to become president — suggesting that the office is something of a 'training ground' — the vice-presidency has, until recently, been seen as something of a joke. Reflecting on his time as vice president, for example, John Nance Garner concluded that the office 'ain't worth a pitcher of warm spit'. More recently, Walter Mondale (Carter's vice president) described the position as 'handmade for ridicule and for dismissal'. Such remarks are not surprising. Since the 1950s, vice-presidential candidates have been chosen by each party's presidential candidate. As Bob Dole remarked in 1991: 'It only takes one vote to win the vice-presidential nomination.' The vice-presidential candidate has, therefore, often been chosen simply to 'balance the ticket' and gain the broadest possible support from within the party and beyond. The relatively inexperienced Bush, therefore, went for the political heavyweight Cheney. Since the pair were elected, however, many have argued that Cheney has become the real 'power behind the throne' — the 'prime minister' to Bush's 'head of state'. If this is true, we could be seeing a significant change in the status of the office. Though former vice presidents have been given specific responsibilities within some administrations (for example, Gore negotiating NAFTA for Clinton), Cheney appears to be playing a far more important role than any other recent vice president.

The candidate provides a clear summary of the roles of the vice president before moving on to consider how the office is perceived. A major strength of this answer is the assured way in which the candidate combines theory with examples and quotations. This is more than sufficient to gain a grade A.

D-grade answer to question 3.2

The US vice president is elected alongside the president as part of the ticket. Every 4 years, in November, voters get to decide who they want in the White House. Like the president, the vice president must be a natural born citizen who has been resident in the USA for at least 14 years prior to the election. They must also be at least 35 years old.

The vice president is there to balance the ticket. If the president is from the north, then the vice president is often from the south. Some less experienced presidential candidates (e.g. George W. Bush) choose a more experienced vice president (e.g. Dick Cheney) to add credibility to their ticket.

The main role of the vice president is to take over if and when the president dies in office or is incapacitated. When Ronald Reagan was shot, George Bush Senior took over for a while and Johnson took over when Kennedy was assassinated.

 There is plenty of accurate material here but the candidate does not address the demands of the question. The focus on the vice president's roles — as opposed to the requirements for office — is limited and there is no explicit discussion of 'importance'.

Question 3.3

Which is of more use to the president — the cabinet or the Executive Office of the President (EXOP)?

(30 minutes)

This question requires you to make a straightforward judgement, but remember that you don't have to make your final judgement totally black and white. You could, for example, argue that the cabinet and EXOP are both of real use to the president, but in different ways. You could also conclude that both bodies are of as much 'use' as the incumbent president chooses to make of them. Whatever conclusion you go for, you are unlikely to score highly unless you demonstrate a clear knowledge and understanding of the nature and roles of both the cabinet and EXOP.

A-grade answer to question 3.3

In 1937 the Brownlow Committee concluded that 'the president needs help'. Its comments reflected the massive expansion in the role of the presidency that had taken place since the time of the constitution. The US cabinet and the Executive Office of the President (EXOP) are two bodies that can offer him some support.

The constitution makes no mention of the cabinet. The institution is therefore largely what the president of the day chooses to make of it. In Britain, the cabinet is drawn from the legislature (in a large part the Commons), but in America the separation of powers prevents members of the executive branch simultaneously holding office in the legislature or the judiciary. Presidents have a free hand to appoint whoever they want. As Harry S. Truman remarked in 1945: 'Everyone is telling me who I should have on my staff and in my cabinet. No S.O.B. is going to dictate to me who I am going to have.' US cabinet members are, however, most often specialists in their field and only about one in five cabinet members have any experience in Congress. Anthony Principi, for example, the Veterans' Affairs Secretary, is a Vietnam veteran.

US cabinet members are therefore not elected but appointed by the president and this means that they are dependent upon him or her. Members must compete for the ear of the president and the president's decision is final. As George Bush Senior told his cabinet nominees in 1989: 'when I make a call, we move as a team.'

Many students can make general comments regarding the role of the US cabinet, but this answer is distinctive because the candidate creates a vivid picture through the clever combination of examples — historic and current — and quotations.

The scale of work undertaken normally means that cabinet members work fairly independently of one another. The president is easily able to 'divide and rule' and the fact that its members have to compete for the president's attention tends to make the cabinet 'a schizophrenic body' (Richard Fenno). Cabinet meetings are still important, however, because they allow members a chance to see one another, give members an opportunity to see the president and facilitate the collection and dissemination of information. Cabinet meetings also allow the resolution of interdepartmental conflicts and a focusing of the collective effort. Ultimately, though, it is what the president thinks that matters. As Ronald Reagan commented: 'When I've heard enough of a debate to satisfy my needs about knowing, then I make a decision.'

The Executive Office of the President (EXOP) is another body that is there to help the president. EXOP consists of three main elements: the White House staff, the National Security Council and the Office of Management and Budget.

Most students avoid tackling questions on the federal bureaucracy because they cannot do what this candidate does in this single sentence, i.e. identify precisely what the federal bureaucracy is. This clear and accurate outline sets up the second half of the essay.

The White House staff includes the president's closest aides and confidants together with those working beneath them. Whereas cabinet members focus on the work of their own departments and have to consider the demands of Congress (who assign their budgets) as well as the president, those in the White House staff are the president's true policy advisors. The roles of press secretary and chief of staff (Ari Fleischer and Andrew Card respectively under George W. Bush) are particularly important. Unless the president has a good chief of staff, who can decide objectively what the president needs to deal with personally and what can be dealt with without wasting the president's valuable time, the president will be buried under an avalanche of paperwork and telephone calls.

The White House staff provides the bulk of the president's policy advice and also helps to coordinate the efforts of the White House with those of the federal bureaucracy and Congress. They also administer the daily round of meetings in the White House.

The National Security Council was created in 1947 and has the role of coordinating policy relating to national security, both domestic and foreign. It is headed by the National Security Advisor (NSA — currently Condoleezza Rice) and includes the president, the vice president, and the secretaries of state and defense, with occasional visits from the CIA head and the chiefs of staff.

The Office of Management and Budget (OMB) was created in 1970 under the control of an OMB director. It has three clear roles: organising the budget, balancing the demands of the various departments and deciding where to wield the axe. It oversees departmental and agency spending and provides on-tap specialist financial backup and advice for the president.

In conclusion, therefore, we can see that both the cabinet and EXOP provide help to the president but that EXOP probably has more influence because it provides more in terms of policy advice. Most cabinet members are more concerned with their own departments and often have a closer day-to-day working relationship with congressional committees and agencies than they do with the president of the day.

🄴 **This answer would achieve full marks for AO1 (knowledge and understanding), and is communicated well (AO3). The overall level of analysis and evaluation (AO2) is also good, though the discussion becomes a little 'bitty' and descriptive towards the end. The conclusion could also be stronger, perhaps recognising that the roles played by both bodies are largely at the whim of the president of the day.**

Topic

The US Supreme Court

Question 4.1

Is the US Supreme Court best seen as a threat to or a defender of democracy in the United States?

(45 minutes)

 In answering this question it is essential to have a good idea of what democracy is. It is not crucial to put a definition of democracy — or your understanding of it in this context — in the introduction, but it might be advantageous. Clearly, no one could defend the composition of the Supreme Court as being democratic. This does not, however, mean that the court itself might not act in the broad interests of democracy by holding democratically elected governments to the US constitution. This is clearly an answer that requires a good level of theoretical and analytical understanding, so you need to think carefully about where your answer is going *before* you start writing.

■ ■ ■

A-grade answer to question 4.1

Over the years, many writers have expressed concerns over the democratic credentials of the US Supreme Court. Much of this concern stems from the fact that the court consists of nine unelected and largely unaccountable men and women with an average age of around 68. Why should this group of nine be able to block the actions of the other two branches of the federal government, both elected at regular intervals by as many US citizens who are over 18 and can be bothered to register and vote? Does the fact that the court is not composed on democratic lines mean that it is in itself a threat to democracy? We must examine the composition of the court more closely and also consider the impact of the court over the years in order to assess the validity of this statement.

 This is a strong introduction, although some kind of definition of democracy might have made life easier later on. An implicit definition appears in the first sentence of the next paragraph, but this could have been made more explicit.

The US Supreme Court cannot be considered a 'democratic institution' in the sense that it is not elected and its members are not accountable in any obvious way to the American people. Though House members, Senators and presidents must put themselves before the voters at regular intervals in order to stay in office, Supreme Court justices are appointed for life. They can only be removed through the impeachment process and this can only be initiated in the event of high crimes or misdemeanours. Only one justice, Samuel Chase, has ever been impeached and he was not convicted, dying in office in 1911. There is some democratic input into the appointment process. The president (who is democratically elected) nominates candidates to fill vacancies in the court, and the Senate (which is democratically elected too) has the role of confirming or rejecting these nominations. That said, there is no direct public input in the selection of Supreme Court justices, unlike many lower US judges who are elected. Clearly, then, the court is not democratic in its composition or selection, but does this mean that it is itself a threat to democracy? It could be argued that it is in the interests of democracy for the USA to have such a body providing an independent check on whether the federal government and the various states are operating within the rules of the constitution. If the Supreme Court were elected, its members would be under direct pressure to make popular decisions in order to get re-elected, even where these decisions required them to twist the constitution to their own ends. This would be much worse for democracy in the long run than having an unelected court that is able to make the decisions that it thinks are right without fear of removal from office. If we look at some of the Supreme Court's actions, we can see just how its members' freedom from election has allowed it to make the really hard decisions.

e The candidate uses a good linking sentence, which opens up the rest of the question.

In the area of civil rights, the court played a central role in the removal of segregation and the assertion of black rights in the USA. 1950s America was divided over race. Many politicians were too scared to grasp the nettle and do what needed to be done because they were worried about their own political careers and what might happen to them if they were seen as the ones who had led calls for change. Because the Supreme Court was unelected, it was able to interpret the constitution and effectively change the law (through the *Brown v. Board of Education, Topeka* case) without having to face an electoral backlash. Ending segregation was a democratic step that the elected elements of government found politically difficult to take. The undemocratically constituted Supreme Court was able to make the democratic change. It is also interesting to see that the court was prepared to update its interpretation of the same passage of the constitution over time (between *Plessy* v. *Ferguson* and *Brown*), thus making the eighteenth-century document relevant to the needs of the time.

Another good example would be 'gerrymandering'. Gerrymandering is where democratically elected bodies deliberately change electoral districts in such a way as to make their own re-election or the re-election of their friends more likely, by leaving more unsympathetic voters in neighbouring constituencies and bringing more sympathetic voters into their own district. Here we have democratically elected bodies doing something that is clearly undemocratic because it makes more marginal seats safer and thus reduces the power of the voter to change the elected representative through the ballot box. Once again, it was the unelected, undemocratically constituted

Supreme Court that declared this practice illegal (unconstitutional) in cases such as *Baker* v. *Carr*.

In *George W. Bush* v. *Al Gore* (2000) we saw the most obvious example of the democratic process coming face-to-face with the 'unelected' and 'unaccountable' court. With the presidential election deadlocked in Florida, it was the court which had to decide what was to be done. Though many accused the court of favouring the Republican candidate Bush (most of the justices were themselves appointed by Reagan or Bush's father), the Supreme Court actually made the correct decision in law — recognising that the Florida Supreme Court instruction for the recount to continue violated both Florida election law (under which the returning officer had lawfully imposed a deadline) and the 14th Amendment to the US constitution. Once the court made its decision, Gore conceded, Bush assumed office and the fiasco was put to one side. It is hard to imagine how any elected body could have resolved a problem of this scale where the most democratic process (the election) appeared to have fallen apart.

In conclusion, I believe that the US Supreme Court has, despite its undemocratic composition, made the survival of the US constitution possible. The court has re-worked the constitution to meet the demands of a developing society through its willingness to change its interpretations on key issues over time. It has given guidance to lower courts when they couldn't agree with one another. It has acted as the ultimate court of appeal for many who were wrongly convicted at lower, less impartial (often elected) levels of the judiciary. It has also led to the reversal of anti-democratic practices (e.g. segregation), when elected bodies seemed unable or unwilling to act decisively. Because it is unelected and unaccountable it can foil the attempts of popularly elected governments to limit individual rights and threaten the spirit of the constitution.

This is an excellent conclusion. It targets the question directly and arrives at a measured and reasoned judgement. The candidate structures the discussion quite effectively, moving from 'democratic in composition' to 'democratic influence through its decisions'. The discussion of *Bush* v. *Gore* (2000) demonstrates a depth of knowledge and understanding uncommon at this level. This would receive a high grade A.

Question 4.2

What controls operate on the US Supreme Court?

(15 minutes)

This is a short, snappy question. Note that it is asking you to identify 'controls' on the court, not powers of the court. Structure your answer accordingly. You might usefully divide your answer into sections dealing with the controls exerted by the other two branches of the federal government — the president and Congress. The answer below goes further still, making a number of very sophisticated points. You would probably not need to go this far in order to achieve a grade A.

■ ■ ■

A-grade answer to question 4.2

Supreme Court justices have an extremely secure tenure. They can only be removed through impeachment as a result of high crimes or misdemeanours and no Supreme Court justice has ever been successfully impeached and removed. Once in office there is little anyone can do to force a justice to make a decision one way or another. As the Supreme Court is the arbiter of the constitution, Congress and the president are expected to respect its decisions regardless of their own views. A number of important congressional and presidential controls can, however, be said to operate on the power of the US Supreme Court.

e This is an extremely purposeful and focused introduction. It provides the answer that follows with context and direction, without using up too much of the limited time available.

Under the US constitution, Congress controls the appellate jurisdiction of the Supreme Court, the number of justices (i.e. the size of the court) and the times when it can sit; in reality, however, these controls are rarely mentioned, let alone exercised.

The president also has one key constitutional check on the court, namely the right to nominate justices to fill vacancies in the court. Yet in reality, the president's power is strictly limited. First, the president can only nominate justices when vacancies occur. Carter, for example, did not appoint any justices, whereas Washington appointed 11 and Franklin D. Roosevelt appointed nine. Second, the president needs the confirmation of the Senate for the nominations and this is not always forthcoming. Nixon had two nominees rejected and Reagan failed in his attempt to get Robert Bork onto the court. Third, the justices do not always live up to the president's expectations, once installed. Eisenhower described his nomination of Chief Justice Earl Warren as 'the biggest damn fool mistake I ever made' and Nixon found that a court including four of his nominees was still prepared to hand over his White House tapes to the Watergate investigation (*US* v. *Nixon*, 1974).

As well as having the power to fill vacancies, presidents can also appeal to Congress to increase the size of the court, thus allowing them to 'pack' it with sympathetic justices. 'Packing' the court is, however, neither quick, nor guaranteed of success. Franklin D. Roosevelt's court-packing bill failed in 1937 but it was enough to persuade one justice, Owen Roberts, to change his position and back the New Deal programme — allowing Roosevelt to carry the court 5:4.

Though the court is under no obligation to listen to the US public and is free from the pressure of re-election, there has always been a feeling amongst US political commentators that the court does keep an 'ear to the ground'. This could, therefore, be seen as some kind of informal 'control'. Public pressure was certainly important at the time that the court backed down over the New Deal and even the *Brown* v. *Board of Education, Topeka* decision (1954) was handed down with strong public support, at least in the north.

In conclusion, the court would be unlikely to survive long unchanged if it persistently acted in a manner directly opposed to the wishes of the people, Congress and the president. After all, with Congress having control of court size and oversight of appellate jurisdiction, and the president's power of appointment checked only by the Senate, the executive and the legislative branches could easily rein in a wayward court.

e **This is a comprehensive answer. The division between presidential controls, congressional controls and the informal 'control' exercised by public opinion works well. The answer scores at the top level on all three Assessment Objectives and would receive a grade A.**

C-grade answer to question 4.2

The only real check on the power of the US Supreme Court is the president. The president has the power to fill vacancies in the court when they arise. Although this power is limited by the fact that the president needs the approval of the Senate, this still gives a real way of controlling the court's actions. If the president's own party controls the Senate, then it probably won't reject presidential nominees anyway. With this power, presidents can appoint justices who share their political outlook. These justices can then make decisions that are in line with the president's policies. Although justices don't always stay loyal to the presidents who appointed them, they normally do. The president can also 'pack' the court. This means that he or she can make the court bigger and then fill it with supporters. Roosevelt tried to do this in the 1930s and it scared the court into letting him get away with many things that were really unconstitutional.

In conclusion, we can see that the president can control the court through appointment.

e **This is a fairly one-dimensional answer. The candidate only discusses presidential controls and, even then, makes a number of statements that do not stand up to close scrutiny. It is also a little on the short side, which is one reason why it lacks depth. Another reason is that the candidate has a fairly low level of understanding.**

Elections and direct democracy

Question 5.1

Examine the part played by primaries and caucuses in the election of US presidents.

(30 minutes)

 Most candidates have a fair appreciation of what primaries are and what role they play. Far fewer candidates are able to explain the part played by caucuses. In order to achieve a grade A for this question, you need to demonstrate a knowledge and understanding of both processes and an awareness of how they differ and the significance of these differences. What you should not do is simply produce a pre-learnt response on the advantages and disadvantages of primaries.

A-grade answer to question 5.1

Primaries and caucuses both occur during the pre-nomination stage in the presidential election season. During this stage members of the public are made aware of the candidates who are seeking the Republican and Democrat nominations, and delegates are chosen who will eventually go to the national party conventions and finalise each party's ticket.

 A good introduction is important here because candidates often become confused over the exact details of the pre-nomination stages.

Primaries are different from caucuses in that they give the broader public a chance to express a preference for one or more of the candidates seeking the party nominations for the presidential election race proper.

 This is not really a paragraph, but it is important in that it draws a clear line between primaries and caucuses, thereby setting the course for what is left of the answer.

Primaries put power into the hands of ordinary voters rather than the party bosses — the 'fat cats' in their 'smoke-filled rooms'. In states using primaries, voters get to say which candidates they think should gain the party's nomination. Their votes are then translated into delegates who attend the party's national convention and make the final decision. In 'open primaries' anyone can vote in either or both of the parties' primaries, but in recent years 'closed primaries' — where only registered supporters of the party can have a say — have become more widespread.

Primaries encourage higher levels of political participation than caucuses because people feel that they can have a real input into the decision-making process. The primaries are very physically and mentally demanding. This is good because it mirrors some of the demands that presidents face in office. Primaries also allow Washington outsiders such as Carter and Clinton to get in on the presidential election act. These individuals might not have been chosen under a system of caucuses, which was used in all states before the emergence of primaries and is still used in a minority of states today.

> It is easy to slip into straightforward description in an essay like this. It is important to remember, however, that the question asks you to 'examine' rather than 'describe'. This candidate makes sure that, at the very least, each paragraph ends with a little analysis or evaluation.

Caucuses leave the power to select delegates with the party activists, who meet first at local, then at county and finally at state level to make their choices. Most states have now moved away from caucuses towards primaries, but some, including Iowa and North Dakota, persevere with caucuses. Some say that this system is better than the primaries because the party bosses, or at least experienced politicians, are better placed to choose candidates than the public. The way in which primaries 'open up the field' is probably beneficial, but we should be wary of seeing 'outsiders' as a 'good thing'. Presidents with inside experience of the federal government are much better placed to achieve legislative success.

Primaries often become straightforward 'beauty contests' and the candidates selected are not necessarily the best for the job — they are simply the lowest common denominator. Of the people who are eligible to vote, only about one in five turn out in primaries. This shows that people don't really take primaries seriously and this undermines the legitimacy of the process. The primary season is also lengthy. With the serious preparation for primaries starting the year before the elections, members of the House are involved in a 'permanent campaign'. Some commentators call this pre-primary campaign the 'invisible primary'. It means that some candidates do not stand because they cannot afford to waste a year or more of their life seeking nomination and then election. The extended campaign season also massively increases the costs of running for president and this means that many worthy but less well-funded candidates drop out early on. This was true of Bill Bradley, who had to withdraw from the Democrat race in 2000 partly for this reason, and Paul Tsongas who had to do the same in 1992.

> **In many respects, this is an impressive answer. The candidate clearly has a lot of factual knowledge and an excellent contextual understanding. However, the structure could have been more effective. Grade-A candidates often move with more direction and fluency towards a reasoned conclusion. The last paragraph in this answer is not really a conclusion at all. Having said that, there is still more than enough here for this candidate to achieve a grade A.**

Question 5.2

Critically examine the role of the Electoral College.

(15 minutes)

e The key to this question is the word 'critically'. You are not simply being asked to describe what the Electoral College is. Instead you must examine its role critically; that is, consider what is wrong with it — both in its conception and in its function. Although a clear outline of what the Electoral College is would be helpful early on, your answer should not stop there.

■ ■ ■

A-grade answer to question 5.2

The Electoral College is a relic of the Founding Fathers' fear of popular power or 'mobocracy'. In all states apart from Maine and Nebraska, the candidate who wins the popular vote in each state receives all of the so-called Electoral College votes assigned to that state. Each state has a number of Electoral College votes equal to the number of Senators it has (two) plus the number of members of the House of Representatives it has (which depends upon the population of the state). Three additional Electors represent the District of Columbia. The Electors (not the actual Congressmen and Senators) chosen to represent the state can then vote for the new president. There are 538 votes in the Electoral College. The winning candidate needs to secure 270 votes in order to become president.

e This candidate takes a factual approach, but as there are only 15 minutes available it is important to address the question immediately. The strength of this approach is that the candidate sets out the origins and workings of the Electoral College clearly and accurately from an early stage. This means that the rest of the answer can focus on the kind of 'critical examination' demanded by the title.

The existence of the Electoral College and its operation have brought a good deal of criticism. First, and most fundamentally, the Electoral College is an anachronism because it was created as a check on the power of the people. Critics argue that this alone makes reform necessary. In fact, there is nothing that can stop Electors from voting for a candidate other than the one they are supposed to vote for. One Elector voted for no one in 2000 and in 1988 one Democratic Elector, who was expected to vote for Dukakis, voted instead for Lloyd Bentsen, who was a Republican.

In addition, it is argued that the college is unfair because a president can be elected with less than 50% of the popular vote. George W. Bush, for example, won 540,000 fewer votes than Gore in 2000, yet still took the White House. This is possible because of the 'winner-takes-all system' operating in most states. A candidate can, therefore, win the larger states — which carry the most Electoral College votes (ECVs) — by a small margin and, at the same time, lose the smaller states by a large margin.

The winner-takes-all system also tends to disadvantage smaller, third-party candidates such as Ross Perot. These candidates gain a significant percentage of the popular vote across the USA, but do not have the concentration of support necessary to win any one state. Perot gained 19% of the vote in 1992 but failed to win a single ECV.

Those who favour the retention of the Electoral College argue that it works effectively and is well understood. The fact that it is an anachronism, they argue, is no reason to replace it. Though the election of the president remains, technically at least, indirect, most Electors in the college vote as instructed by their states and many are bound by legal contract. In reality, the college is little more than a rubber stamp and it rarely makes any difference to the outcome of the election.

The fact that the college promotes a two-horse race means that the winning president can normally claim the support of 50% of the voters. Though the Electoral College disadvantages third-party candidates such as Perot, they are never going to win anyway unless they can amass a high level of national support.

🄴 **This is a fairly long answer given the time available. The candidate writes fluently and with purpose, demonstrating a clear understanding of what the Electoral College is and how it works. A number of problems that arise from its operation are dealt with clearly and thoughtfully. This answer would achieve a high grade A.**

■ ■ ■

C/D-grade answer to question 5.2

The Electoral College consists of 538 votes. In order to win the presidential election, a candidate must get more than half of these votes (i.e. 270). The college never meets as such — the votes are sent from each state and the result is then announced. Each state has a number of Electoral College votes equal to the total number of Congressmen (House plus Senate).

The candidate who wins the most votes in each state wins all of the Electoral College votes for that state. The candidates have to win as many states as they can if they want to be president. The large states like California and Florida have a lot more Electoral College votes than the smaller states, such as Alaska and Maine.

When the Electors cast their Electoral College votes they are choosing the president, not the ordinary American voters. This system is a relic of the past, when the Founding Fathers didn't trust the people to vote for the president directly.

🄴 **The material presented here is fairly accurate but the candidate does little to target the question. The title requires a critical examination of the role of the**

Electoral College, but this candidate only describes the role and composition of the college without any critical analysis or evaluation.

■ ■ ■

Question 5.3

In what way(s) is an initiative different from a referendum?

(10 minutes)

 This is the shortest question that you can face at A2. In 10 minutes, you only really have time to get down the most direct of definitions along with an illustrative example or two. Do not allow yourself to become 'bogged down' in a lengthy discussion of the merits and demerits of each mechanism. This will only use up time that you need later on for higher-mark questions. On AQA Module 5 this question would be part (a) of the compulsory question. It is therefore vital to have a clear knowledge and understanding of the difference between these two mechanisms. In a question such as this, it is important to give definitions that are specific to the country in question (in this case the USA) rather than generic dictionary definitions or definitions remembered from your AS course (which was probably UK specific).

■ ■ ■

A-grade answer to question 5.3

A referendum is a popular vote on a measure proposed or passed by a legislature (as opposed to a measure proposed by the people). Referendums generally take place where: the legislature decides to put a measure or policy to a public vote; the legislature is required by law to put certain measures to a public vote; or the people have the right to force a referendum on a law passed by the legislature by raising a petition carrying a predetermined number of signatures. This is often known as a petition referendum. A recent example is Proposition 47 in California (2002), which aimed to raise $13 billion to provide new schools and repair existing educational establishments.

Initiatives differ from referendums in that they allow voters to propose (initiate) laws themselves from scratch. They operate — in one form or another — in 24 states. The normal procedure is that those proposing the law must produce a petition carrying the support of a predetermined percentage of the population (normally between 5% and 15%) in order for it to qualify. Once qualified, the issue will be placed on the ballot automatically (in some states) or via the legislature (in others). Registered voters in the state then have the chance to vote on the proposal, and the measure either becomes law or falls. A good example would be Proposition 49 in California (2002). This initiative was sponsored by Arnold Schwarzenegger and aimed to provide before and after school programmes, offering students tutoring and help with homework.

 There is only time here to provide clear definitions and, if possible, illustrate with an example or two. This response would gain a grade A, as it covers these points fluently in the time available.

C-grade answer to question 5.3

An initiative is different from a referendum in one important way. With a referendum, voters are asked to give their verdict on a change or proposal that is put forward by the government. It is the government which writes the law and the government which chooses whether or not and when to ask the question. With an initiative, voters themselves have the power to write their own proposals and then force a public vote on them. This means that initiatives really give the people the power to make law without the legislature's approval.

 This is a concise and focused answer. It is not strictly correct that the government always gets to choose whether or not or when to call referendums, as many US state constitutions require referendums when the state legislature passes certain kinds of measure (for example, raising bonds or amending the state constitution). The candidate recognises the fundamental difference between these two devices, but the answer is a little superficial and there are no examples.

Question 5.4

Evaluate the use of initiatives and referendums in the US context.

(30 minutes)

 This question requires you to take your knowledge and understanding of initiatives and referendums a step further. The word 'evaluate' means that you must assess how these devices work in practice, not just in theory. What benefits do they bring and at what cost? A grade-A response would include some examples, though they wouldn't have to be as up-to-date as the ones provided in the answer below. There are lots of excellent historic examples (Proposition 13 in California, for example) and you can find these in most A-level textbooks.

A-grade answer to question 5.4

Although no provision exists in the US constitution for nation-wide referendums, many US states employ devices that allow a degree of state-wide, county-wide or local direct democracy. Essentially, a referendum is a public vote, initiated by the government, authorising or legitimising a particular course of action. An initiative, in contrast, is a mechanism that allows a predetermined number of voters to sign a petition that puts a question on a ballot paper proposing new legislation. Thus referendums let the voters pass judgement on government proposals, whereas initiatives allow them to come up with their own proposals.

🄴 Once again, it is important to get clear definitions in place from the outset as this paragraph does.

A wide range of such devices are operated by US states and an equally broad range of issues are tested by them. In Nevada in November 2000, for example, voters were asked whether or not they wanted to ban gay marriage and legalise cannabis at the same time as they were casting their votes for US president, one of the state's Senators, their House members, members of the state legislature and other elected officials. At the same time, voters in Oregon and Colorado were balloted on whether or not their states should introduce background checks at gun shows. This essay will look specifically at how referendums and initiatives operate in the state of California, before making some general points about the merits and demerits of such mechanisms in a broader sense.

🄴 This paragraph is important, not primarily for the examples, but for its final sentence. Although some candidates may prefer not to write in a style as direct as this, this sentence clearly sets out the scope of the discussion ahead. This makes it far less likely that the candidate's answer will drift too far from the question.

The Californian state legislature is required by law to put certain measures to referendum before they can be enacted. Two of the most common measures are legislative bond measures (any bill that involves expenditure requiring the issuing of bonds) and legislative constitutional amendments (any bill that proposes an amendment to the Californian state constitution). Both types of measures must be adopted in each house of the state legislature (Assembly and Senate) by a two-thirds majority. Legislative bond measures must then be approved by the state governor before moving to a public referendum where a simple majority is required in order for the measure to be enacted. Legislative constitutional amendments passed by the state legislature go straight to public referendum — again requiring a simple majority — without the need for gubernatorial approval. In November 2002, for example, a referendum (Proposition 48) was called to approve a legislative constitutional amendment aimed at consolidating different levels of the state judiciary.

Initiatives differ from referendums in that they allow voters to propose (initiate) laws themselves. They operate — in one form or another — in 24 states. Under the

Californian regulations, a state-wide initiative must qualify to be placed on the ballot at least 131 days before the next state-wide election. In order to qualify, initiatives proposing changes in statute must have a number of signatures equal to 5% of the total number of votes cast for the governor in the previous gubernatorial election. In November 2002 the target to qualify an initiative was therefore a petition carrying 419,260 votes. The bar is set somewhat higher for those wishing to initiate an amendment to the state's constitution (8% or 670,816 signatures in November 2002). Signatories to the petition must be registered, qualified voters and they have to sign in their own county. Following the petition deadline, counties forward their totals to the Californian secretary of state. Samples of signatures are then checked before the measure is certified and put on the ballot. In November 2002, for example, the initiative known as Proposition 52, which aimed to allow election-day voter registration, was rejected by the voters.

e The material provided here is excellent, though these two paragraphs are rather content-heavy, and would benefit from a balance between description and analysis.

Such referendums and initiatives clearly offer citizens a greater degree of 'direct democracy'. They can have a real input into key decisions, thereby encouraging political participation. Such mechanisms also provide a way of legitimising major changes that may have an impact far beyond the term of a state legislature. That said, such mechanisms are inconsistent with the principles of a representative democracy. Referendums and initiatives can create a tyranny of the majority, or even of a committed minority where turnout is low. Far from encouraging participation, regular use of such measures can lead to apathy and cynicism. This in turn can lead to low turnouts that might distort the results. It is also said that most issues are simply too complicated to be condensed into a simple 'yes/no' question.

e **This is clearly a grade-A answer, although the candidate could have dispensed with some of the peripheral detail in favour of a little more analysis and evaluation. The last paragraph, ironically, contains a lot of good theory and analysis but could have been brought to life with one or two illustrative examples.**

Political culture and voting behaviour

Question 6.1

Why do so many US voters 'split their tickets' when voting in presidential and congressional elections and what are the consequences of such behaviour?

(45 minutes)

Definitions are central to answering this question effectively. The term 'split-ticket voting' refers to a very specific kind of voting behaviour, i.e. when voters decide to cast their votes in favour of candidates representing different parties, for different offices in the same electoral session. On the same day in 2000, for example, voters in some states may have supported Republican George W. Bush for president yet at the same time voted for a Democrat as their Senator. The term should *not* be used to describe a situation in which, for example, someone voted for Republican George W. Bush in 2000 but then voted for a Democrat Senator in 2002. This is not split-ticket voting because there was no opportunity to vote for the president in 2002. Getting the definition wrong in this way can result in wasting a lot of time in the examination on material that is not creditable. A clear definition at the start can get your answer off on the right foot.

■ ■ ■

A-grade answer to question 6.1

Because there are so many elected offices in the United States, American voters often find themselves being asked to choose representatives for a wide range of positions, at various levels of government, on the same day. In November 2000 some Americans voted for their choice of president, one of their Senators, their district's member of the House of Representatives, their state governor, state legislators, judges and so on. 'Split-ticket voting' occurs when voters choose to cast their vote for candidates from different parties on a single election day like this. For example, they might vote for a Republican president, but a Democrat governor and a Democrat Senator. Why do they do this?

This is a good introduction. The candidate gives as sound a definition as can be expected in test conditions and sets up the focus of the next paragraph in the last sentence.

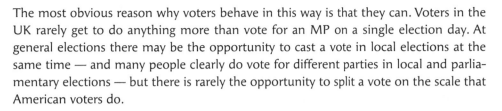

The most obvious reason why voters behave in this way is that they can. Voters in the UK rarely get to do anything more than vote for an MP on a single election day. At general elections there may be the opportunity to cast a vote in local elections at the same time — and many people clearly do vote for different parties in local and parliamentary elections — but there is rarely the opportunity to split a vote on the scale that American voters do.

The second reason for split-ticket voting is the ideological weakness of US political parties compared to those in the UK. In America the parties are so similar that voters are less likely to have a problem in voting for candidates from different parties on the same day. Democrat candidates in the south often have far more in common ideologically with Republicans in the south than they do with their northern Democratic colleagues. Accordingly, it has been said that US political parties have more differences within them than between them. Strom Thurmond, who served in the Senate until January 2003, was one of the most right-wing people in Congress in the 1950s and 1960s, yet he started as a Democrat. Only later did he switch to the Republican Party. Ironically, he was less right-wing as a Republican in 2003 than he was as a Democrat earlier in his career. The last time that he was elected (in 1996), he even managed to win around 20% of the black vote.

Because the parties are ideologically weak, the candidates themselves become more important. As a result, voters might split their tickets because they want to vote for a particularly good Democrat for governor, even though they are likely to vote Republican in most of the other contests being held on the same day. Clinton won many traditionally Republican states in 1992 and 1996 because he was able to appeal to many moderate Republican voters. This is because he was a 'New Democrat' who distanced himself from the tax-and-spend policies of liberal Democrats. In 1996, Clinton was returned as president at the same time as the Republicans had control of the House and the Senate. Strom Thurmond was elected as a Democrat and as a Republican in the same state because people voted for the man rather than his party.

Another reason why some US voters split their tickets is because they are making real decisions about the kind of government they want. Some voters believe that Republicans make good presidents because they are tough on foreign policy, but prefer the Democrats to be in control of Congress. Many voters like the idea of a White House controlled by one party having to fight it out with a Congress controlled by another. They believe that this divided government prevents any one branch from having too much control.

These are four key reasons why American voters split their tickets, but what are the consequences of such voting behaviour? The main consequence of split-ticket voting on a large scale is said to be the kind of divided government outlined above. For some, this is advantageous because Congress and the president then have to stand up for themselves and use their constitutional powers to control the other effectively. However, some people see divided government as a problem. Deeply divided government can lead to so-called 'gridlock', where the two branches of government dig in their heels and nothing can get done. Reagan, for example, had problems getting his budget through in the 1980s due to the Democrat control of the House. Clinton faced similar problems in 1995 too, after the 1994 mid-term election had left the Republicans in charge of the House. We should remember, however, that Clinton's health reform plans were defeated by a Democrat-controlled House and Senate in 1993 and Carter (a Democrat) also had to appeal to Republicans in Congress to pass his federal bureaucracy cost-cutting plans after Democrat House members opposed them. Though divided government can lead to gridlock, therefore, presidents can face just as many problems when their own party is in control of Congress.

 This answer begins with an excellent introduction and then provides four developed and plausible reasons why US voters might split their tickets. Unsurprisingly, perhaps, the candidate is unable to deal with the 'consequences' part of the question in as much depth, and there is no formal conclusion, but this is still a grade-A answer.

■ ■ ■

Question 6.2

'Poor people can't be elected now' (Raymond Strother). Is money the most important factor in determining the outcome of presidential and congressional elections?

(45 minutes)

 Although this question focuses on the importance of money in elections, you cannot talk about the influence of money alone. In order to decide which is the most important factor, you must discuss other factors too. The key to a good answer is, therefore, first to write a detailed paragraph dealing with the influence of money. Second, identify a number of factors other than money (e.g. candidate image, policies, party label). Third, write one detailed paragraph on the influence of each additional factor that you have identified. Finally, come to a balanced conclusion as to whether or not money is indeed the most important factor of those that you have dealt with.

■ ■ ■

A-grade answer to question 6.2

In February 2003 it was reported that George W. Bush had amassed an election 'war chest' of over $100 million ahead of the 2004 primary season. His position as incumbent president and his links with the oil industry and big business in general make him a magnet for large campaign contributions. While Strother is wrong to say that poor people *can't* be elected, the fact that Bush already had this much money ready for a campaign that was still over a year away would suggest that a poor candidate will find it difficult to compete.

> 🄴 This paragraph starts off with an impressive and relevant example, before moving on to make some general introductory remarks about the proposition in the title. The candidate could have provided a more obvious agenda for the discussion to come, but this is still a perfectly adequate opening gambit.

There are a number of reasons why money has become so important in presidential and congressional elections. First, candidates need to produce adverts and buy airtime. This is very expensive. Some estimate that 3 minutes of airtime can cost as much as $30,000. Though candidates can take advantage of unpaid media coverage — news programmes, chat shows, debates etc. — they need to be prepared to buy slots on prime-time television because paid coverage can be controlled much more easily. Some candidates use this time to broadcast biographical advertisements, which aim to tell voters something about the candidate's life and to put a face to a name.

A good example is the advert by Frank Greer that helped Gaston Caperton III become Governor of West Virginia in 1988, despite his obvious lack of political experience. In a country of 290 million people and with states such as California having populations of around 30 million, the only way to achieve good name recognition is through measures such as this.

Once candidates have gained name recognition, they may adopt more subtle tactics by using subliminal adverts. These rarely mention the candidate but instead focus on creating a positive mood and allowing voters to make their own connections, an example being the 'It's Morning in America' adverts deployed by Reagan's team in 1984. For those candidates for whom money is no object, the sky is the limit. Ross Perot spent $2 million per day in the latter stages of the campaign buying up 30-minute television slots and then broadcasting lengthy party political programmes ('infomercials') that he presented himself. Paid advertising is an essential and expensive part of both congressional and presidential campaigns. The rise of negative 'attack-ads' has further increased the cost of the campaigns because negative attacks have to be answered with either more attack-ads or adverts promoting the candidate's good character.

> 🄴 This section contains plenty of accurate examples. It provides more than is needed for a grade A, and risks focusing too much on one area at the expense of the remainder of the essay.

There are numerous other costs associated with the campaign. These can add up to a huge total, encompassing: costs of travelling (not just for candidates but for their campaign teams too); acquiring office space and office staff (offices cost money and not all staff are volunteers); setting up phone-lines and handling donations; issuing mail-shots (sending out information to the voters); coordinating merchandising (shirts, banners, badges, mugs etc.).

All of these costs have been made worse by the increasing length of the contests. The emergence of primaries over the older system of caucuses in many states has meant that candidates now have to fight a campaign that is well over a year long, with the November election simply being the final act. House members, elected every 2 years, are effectively in a state of permanent campaign. They never have a chance to reflect on their election victory. They are constantly compelled to think about the next primary. This permanent campaign costs money. Presidential candidates also have to face primaries at the start of election year, but the campaign starts much earlier than that. Many commentators speak of the 'invisible primary' — the campaign leading up to the primaries themselves — during which the candidates try to gain name recognition and position themselves for the race itself. Many presidential candidates declare their interest and start campaigning years before the election itself. By the start of 2003 there were already a handful of serious Democratic hopefuls on the circuit trying to raise money for the 2004 elections.

All of these factors have created an enormous demand for cash and this demand has been met by the rise of Political Action Committees (PACs). Some argue that PACs actually increase the cost of elections themselves by offering money to one candidate, whereupon the other candidate immediately needs to start thinking about raising money to balance this.

Even in 1992 the average incumbent in the House spent $580,000 on a re-election campaign. In the presidential campaign of the same year, the independent Ross Perot spent $23.9 million, of which nearly all was his own money. Spending money does not, of course, guarantee success. Perot lost in 1992 and in 1996 when he spent more than the federal limit (over $50 million of his own money) for matching funds. Michael Huffington spent $26 million trying to win a Senate seat (California) in 1994 and still lost to incumbent Dianne Feinstein. If not money alone, then what other factors determine the outcome of presidential and congressional elections?

It is a fact that incumbents tend to win re-election when they seek it. In 2000, 98% of House members seeking re-election won, as did 83% of similarly placed Senators. Is this because people tend to vote for experience or because incumbents receive 75% of PAC funding and can, therefore, run more powerful campaigns? Does money win the election for a candidate or does the money simply follow the candidate who is likely to win (and end up in power)?

The 'party label' appears to matter too. All but two House members and one Senator were Republican or Democrat before the 2002 mid-terms. However weak the parties are, therefore, it is clearly important to have a party label if you want to win — something that probably worked against Perot.

Image is of key importance (Perot might have suffered in this area as well). Candidates need to look good and come across well on television. Many commentators question whether presidents such as Lincoln or Roosevelt would be able to get elected in today's political climate because of their physical appearance (looks in Lincoln's case, disability in Roosevelt's).

Candidates who are too extreme are also unlikely to get elected. Pat Buchanan, for example, who was first a Republican hopeful and then a Reform Party candidate, was too right wing for many voters.

> This section on 'other factors' looks like something of an afterthought but there are some strong points here. By spending rather less time looking at the influence of money, the candidate might have been able to deal with these other factors rather more thoroughly.

Money is not, therefore, the only important factor, but it nearly always helps raise a candidate's profile, and it is difficult for a candidate to stay on the campaign trail for over a year and hold down a job. Though the appearance of the candidate and his or her message is also important, voters never see or hear a candidate unless the candidate has the funds to pay for the adverts that gain him or her name-recognition. You cannot elect just anyone with money, but you cannot elect anyone without it. Poor people can be elected, but only if they have very rich friends.

> **This is a very strong conclusion. The point about the candidate's message being lost without the funds to broadcast it is a particularly sophisticated one. This response would be awarded a grade A.**

Question 6.3

Explain the reasons for such low turnouts in US elections.

(15 minutes)

> Again, this answer needs to be short and to the point because of the limited time available. Avoid writing a lengthy introduction. Instead, give a brief definition of turnout, outline the scale of the problem (preferably with figures) and then deal with two or three reasons for low turnout as quickly as you can.

A-grade answer to question 6.3

Turnout in US elections is measured as a percentage of voting age population (VAP), i.e. the total number of people in the United States who are 18 years of age or older regardless of citizenship, military status, felony conviction or mental state. This definition of turnout creates a number of problems. First, not everyone of voting age is entitled to vote. A large number are not US citizens. Second, many of those who are entitled to vote are not registered to vote, so they have no way of turning out to vote in their state.

e This is a valid way into the question and the central point made here is an important one. If you were short of time, however, you could probably start at the next paragraph without affecting your mark significantly.

As a result, turnout figures in presidential and particularly in congressional elections are often very low indeed. For example, when measured as a percentage of VAP, turnout was only 51.3% in the 2000 presidential election. If we measure turnout as a percentage of those who were registered to vote, then the figure for 2000 would have been 68%. Clearly, whichever measure we take, turnout in US elections is still low, even though Election Day is a national holiday. There are several reasons for this.

First, as mentioned above, there is a real problem with voter registration in some areas, particularly among those who are poorer and/or less educated. Historically, this has meant that lots of black Americans have not been registered — a fact that was addressed by the voter registration drives started in these communities by politicians such as Jesse Jackson in the 1980s. If people don't register to vote, then, in many states, they will not be able to vote on Election Day. Some states allow election-day registration (e.g. Idaho) and more are doing so since the National Voter Registration Act (NVRA) took effect in 1995. This act, known as the 'motor voter' law, required states to make registration available at facilities more easily accessible to voters.

Second, many commentators have identified a degree of apathy amongst the US electorate. Some voters clearly feel that government is not for them. Only around 27% of Hispanic voters voted in 2000, for example. Perhaps this is because candidates are predominantly male, rich, white and well educated. In 2002 only 13% of the House of Representatives was black or Hispanic and there were no black or Hispanic Senators. Neither of the two main political parties has ever nominated a black presidential or vice-presidential candidate and only the Democrats have ever put a woman on the ticket (Geraldine Ferraro for vice president in 1984).

Some Americans may feel that whoever they vote for, the outcome will be the same because the two parties are so similar. Voters feel disengaged and instead participate in other kinds of political activity such as interest group campaigns or direct action.

e **The response starts well with a clear definition and goes on to provide two developed paragraphs dealing with factors that might result in low turnouts. This is a focused and fluent answer which would gain a grade A.**

■ ■ ■

C-grade answer to question 6.3

The main reason why there is such low turnout in the USA is apathy. Most people in America just can't be bothered to vote. Why is this? Well, for most people, government is not relevant to them. They see all of these white, middle-aged men in Congress and think, 'Congress has nothing to do with me'. In 2002 there were no blacks or Hispanics in the Senate but over half of all Senators were lawyers. This is hardly a cross-section of America, is it? Voters might also look at the presidential candidates and see the same problem. No non-white candidate has ever won the nomination for either of the big two parties. In fact, only one woman has ever made it onto the ticket (with Mondale) and they got massacred. Some people think that Hillary Clinton might stand as the Democratic candidate in 2004 or 2008. That would be good. A woman would appeal to female voters who don't vote and that would be better for turnout. Also, lots of people don't vote because they are not registered and this is because they are too stupid and do not understand the form or they don't have time to fill them in or they have better things to do. Even the ones that do vote are often too stupid to vote properly. In Florida in 2000 many voters couldn't even punch a hole right through a piece of paper!

The style of this answer does the candidate a disservice. There are several good points here, but the inappropriate style obscures the argument in places. The answer also lacks depth and would gain no more than a grade C.

Political parties

Question 7.1

To what extent is it true to say that third parties are doomed to failure?

(30 minutes)

 To tackle this question effectively you need background knowledge of recent and historic third party candidatures (e.g. Wallace, Perot, Nader) as well as a good understanding of how the electoral system works (e.g. the Electoral College and the winner-takes-all system) and the nature of the US party system (the importance of being a 'broad church', for example). An understanding of key institutions and processes will help you explain why the odds are so stacked against minor parties. Having an awareness of recent third party candidatures will give you a range of examples.

■ ■ ■

A-grade answer to question 7.1

There have been two major political parties in the USA from the time of Jefferson, though the names have changed over the years. This is partly the result of a natural need for a clear, two-way choice and partly a result of the electoral system, which makes it difficult for third parties to make a breakthrough.

 This is a reasonable opening paragraph, though an introduction should, ideally, set out the scope of the discussion to follow.

Since the constitution was drafted there has been a series of issues and debates that polarised American opinion through time. These include: the issue of ratifying the constitution; the interests of the industrial/financial north versus the agricultural south; anti-slavery versus pro-slavery; and (after the New Deal) the Democrats representing the 'common man' and the Republicans representing 'business'. In a polarised debate, against two parties with established positions, it is often difficult for third parties to carve out a clear and distinct position.

The nature of American society has a part to play too. America is so varied in every way (climate, geography, population etc.) that political parties have to be fairly 'broad churches' if they are to stand any chance of winning large national contests — the race for the White House, or gaining enough seats in the legislature to hold control. The main two parties tend to have broad and uncontroversial platforms in order to capture as many votes as possible. Though they may be divided on some key issues (outlined above), they are often said to have more differences within them than between them. With the two main parties taking such a mainstream position, third parties often have to adopt more extreme policies. This makes them unelectable. If third-party candidates do hit upon a policy which has a broad appeal and has been missed by the other two, the 'big two' often pick the policy up — thereby reinforcing their own positions and undermining the third-party candidate. This happened with Perot's call for better financial management and budget-balancing after 1992.

> **e** The point about the two main parties being 'broad churches' is expressed well. The discussion about the way in which the big two adopt the policies of successful third-party candidates in order to maintain their hegemony is also impressive. This candidate is clearly well informed.

The electoral mechanism also makes it difficult for third-party candidates to make a large impact. Such candidates rarely have the name recognition necessary to gain the winning votes in a first-past-the-post contest. It is an advantage for a candidate to have a big-party label because it means that voters can work out roughly where the candidate is coming from, even if they don't know who the candidate is. The Electoral College also makes it difficult for third-party candidates to win the presidential election because they nearly always have to win a whole state in order to get any of its Electoral College votes (ECVs). Third parties either tend to have their support spread over the whole US — thus winning no Electoral College votes (e.g. Perot, who got 19% of the votes in 1992 and won no ECVs), or have their support concentrated in one area — thus winning one or two states' Electoral College votes but having no chance of picking up the 270 necessary to win the contest (e.g. Wallace, who won 13% of the vote nationally and 46 ECVs).

The cost of the modern election and the extent to which there is now a permanent campaign also makes it hard for all but the richest of third-party candidates to consider a serious race for the White House or even for Congress. In addition, most third parties cannot meet the requirements for them to receive federal matching funds. In many states, complicated rules make it difficult for third-party candidates even to get their names on the ballot.

Despite all of this, third parties can make a difference. They can affect the outcome of the election in a number of ways, even if they do not win. One way in which they can do this is by depriving the major parties of votes. In Florida in 2000, for example, Ralph Nader secured 87,974 votes on the first count. The original margin between Bush and Gore was only 1,784 votes. Nader voters would have been unlikely to vote for Bush had their man not stood, so it could be argued that Nader's candidacy handed the presidency to Bush. By winning even a handful of ECVs, third parties could also prevent a major party achieving a winning 270.

> **e** This answer is put together well. The candidate identifies in turn a number of factors that make it difficult for third parties to break through, and deals with each factor thoroughly. Though the essay is realistically downbeat

about the prospect facing third parties, the final paragraph provides a good contrast. Though it is usual to avoid introducing new ideas or arguments into a conclusion, the quality of the point made is undeniable.

■ ■ ■

Question 7.2

'Some politicians are Republican, some Democratic and their feud is dramatic, but except for the name they are identically the same' (Ogden Nash). How accurate is this assessment of US political parties?

(45 minutes)

e Questions about the differences between the two main parties are relatively common on exam papers. The fact that the USA has two political parties suggests that there must be some differences between them, however small. In your answer, therefore, you could try to identify similarities and differences in nature, organisation, outlook and platforms. A good starting-point might be the nature of American society and the way in which parties have to become 'big umbrellas' or 'broad churches' in order to succeed. Another starting-point might be the Founding Fathers' mistrust of parties and their attempts to pose difficulties for them when framing the US constitution.

A-grade answer to question 7.2

The Founding Fathers were suspicious of political parties; as George Washington observed: 'Parties serve to organise faction; to put in place of the delegated will of the nation, the will of a party.' The constitution was therefore designed to break up rather than unite political power through its institutionalisation of the separation of powers and of checks and balances. The emergence of political parties was something that the Founding Fathers probably never envisaged and certainly never intended.

e The candidate uses the quotation from Washington to good effect here. There are three key points to remember when using quotations: keep them brief; make sure that they are from an authoritative source; and only use them to introduce your argument, to illustrate it or to back it up. The candidate passes all three tests here.

It was, however, the very fact that many Americans had so little in common that made the parties such an attractive proposition. With so much immigration during the early years of the new constitution, political parties gave many Americans something to belong to and provided practical help; they offered a safety net for those facing hard times. As a result, parties quickly took control of the political organisation of many regions and, in particular, cities.

Despite controlling all of this power, however, the parties were still essentially local institutions: they came together once every 4 years for the presidential election but, win or lose, the national party was a 'bloodless skeleton' (H. G. Nicholas) in the meantime. Indeed, parties were decentralised not only to a state but also to a city or county level. At a national level, US political parties had and still have to be broad churches in order to be elected. The result is a situation in which the two parties often appear to have more entrenched differences within them than between them. This is what Ogden Nash referred to in the quotation given in the question. More recently, Mark Shields drew a similar conclusion, arguing that America 'basically has two Republican parties, separated by the issue of abortion'. Is this really true? What differences are there between the two parties — what do they stand for?

For most of the twentieth century the Democratic Party had the broadest possible range of support, being popular in the south and also among ethnic minorities. In the latter half of the twentieth century the Democratic Party came to be associated with 'big government' because it favoured higher levels of taxation and higher spending on education and welfare (particularly the Medicare and Medicaid programmes). This emphasis has meant that it has also been seen as the party of 'the common man'. The Democrats are, therefore, associated with the needy rather than with big business. This may be why they have been the party of choice for lower-income groups and ethnic minorities.

The Democratic Party has also been associated with a more liberal social policy (e.g. pro-choice on the issue of abortion). This may help to explain why it is more popular amongst women. In foreign policy, the Democrats have a reputation for being more 'doves' than 'hawks'. They are keen to get involved in world affairs but favour international organisations and diplomacy over military action.

The Republicans, in contrast, have traditionally been seen as the more conservative of the two parties. Both Reagan (in 1980 and 1984) and Bush Senior (1988) ran on platforms promising low personal taxation. During the 1980s the Republican Party also became associated with the 'New Right' and with right-wing evangelical groups such as Jerry Falwell's 'Moral Majority', which held anti-abortion and anti-gay beliefs. From the time of the New Deal, the Republican Party came to be associated with 'small government' — lower levels of taxation and lower spending on education and welfare. Instead, the party encourages the private sector and entrepreneurial activity. This emphasis has meant that it has been seen as the party of 'big business'. The party favours a degree of 'deregulation' and this often marginalises the rights of individual workers. In large part this means that the Republicans have been supported by those in higher income groups, and — partly as a result of this and partly as a result of their conservative social policies — by 'white' American Protestants (WASPs).

The Republicans are more conservative on social policy (e.g. pro-school prayers, pro-life on the issue of abortion). This may help to explain why they are less popular among women. In foreign policy, the Republicans have a reputation for being more 'hawks' than 'doves'. They are reluctant to get involved in world affairs, preferring a more isolationist stance. When they do get involved, however, they often favour military action over diplomacy through international organisations.

> *e* These paragraphs outlining the two main parties' broad perspectives on key issues are executed well. The overall effect is to make it clear that the two parties may well have more to separate them than name alone.

Despite these generalisations, both parties are very broad churches. The words 'Democrat' and 'Republican' both disguise a massive range of ideas.

The word 'Democrat' really means very little without the addition of a qualifying prefix ('liberal', 'conservative' etc.). Clinton was able to maintain a broad base of support for the party by appealing to independent voters who would normally be fearful of the Democrats' reputation for extensive government welfare programmes and higher taxation. In the 2000 election, some of Gore's speeches were too left-wing for these groups. They were fearful that he would burden them with tax increases aimed at helping lower-income groups.

George W. Bush, in contrast, adopted a more inclusive approach in an attempt to broaden the appeal of the Republican Party and return it to the White House. He adopted the phrase 'compassionate conservatism' and pushed more extreme members of the party (the anti-abortionist Henry Hyde, for example) to the fringes of the party convention.

Writers such as James McGregor Burns have suggested that rather than simply talking about Republicans and Democrats, we should dig a little deeper. In McGregor Burns' argument, Republicans from rural areas have more in common with Democrats from rural areas than they do with their urban Republican 'brothers'. Democrats from urban areas, in contrast, might align with Republicans from districts facing similar social problems in order to support presidents trying to force through policies that will help these areas. Others have drawn a distinction between 'liberal Democrats' (such as Barbara Boxer), 'conservative Democrats' (such as John Breaux), 'moderate' and 'conservative Republicans' (Olympia Snowe and former Senator Jesse Helms respectively).

Though Nash's comments have some basis in truth, therefore, the situation is rather more complex than his comments would suggest.

> *e* **A more comprehensive conclusion would have made this a more secure grade A, but it is nonetheless an excellent response, both in terms of theory and in terms of supporting content.**

Pressure groups

Question 8.1

Assess the view that pressure groups are too powerful in the USA.

(30 minutes)

Although the question does not ask you simply to run through the good and bad points about pressure groups, the task of deciding whether or not US pressure groups are too powerful might lend itself to such an approach. It is important to make sure that your answer does not become too theoretical — you need to keep the right balance between pressure group theory and supporting examples from the USA.

B-grade answer to question 8.1

Pressure groups occur naturally under any system of government. People have a natural desire to unite in protection of their own interests or in advancing a particular cause. Pressure groups are particularly necessary in the USA because America is a hetero-geneous society with a wide range of views and interests. It would be impossible for any political party to represent the full range of opinions effectively. This is what pluralism is about — the ability of different groups and interests to compete openly for the available resources. Groups also play an essential role in moderating the views of their more extreme members. People with such views are, therefore, allowed to 'let off steam' without becoming disaffected and adopting very extreme methods. Without such groups, individuals with extreme views might never have their views challenged and moderated.

This candidate clearly has a good understanding, but is in danger of allowing the response to become too theoretical. It is crucial to apply a theoretical under-standing to the US context.

Pressure groups allow a greater degree of public participation in the political process, particularly between elections when governments can become complacent. Groups play a vital role in educating the general public too. Many necessary changes have been brought about as a result of public pressure resulting from the activities of pressure groups in raising awareness of issues.

Groups provide valuable information to governments. Governments must have access to the best possible information on which to base policy. Pressure groups are often in a position to provide detailed information on specific issues because they tend to be specialised. Many groups also have significant research programmes. At the same time, groups can hold the government accountable. They can act as watchdogs, monitoring the impact of policies and bringing public pressure to bear when governments fail to live up to their promises or their obligations under the law.

Despite all of these obvious benefits, some commentators feel that pressure groups, far from enhancing democracy, actually threaten it. Some groups are far more powerful than others. C. Wright Mills wrote of a 'power elite — the domination of the whole political system and indeed of the entire upper echelon of society by an elite group of people dedicated to preserving their own interests. Many groups are severely disadvantaged by a lack of financial influence. It is difficult, for example, for groups representing poorer people to compete with groups representing business interests. Human resources are an issue too. Groups tend to be more successful if they have articulate, educated leading members. Many have argued that this tends to favour groups run by the middle classes over those set up by the working class for the working class.

Well-resourced and articulate groups, therefore, often have an effect on government that is disproportionate to their size (in terms of number of members). By using direct action, even illegal tactics, groups can defeat the efforts of popularly elected governments and change policy. This has been apparent over abortion, where anti-abortion groups have used intimidation at clinics and have deliberately jammed free-phone lines in order to shut abortion facilities that are operating totally within the law.

e The candidate finally uses some examples in this paragraph.

Some groups also have worryingly close contacts with government. In the case of Enron, for example, leading members of the federal executive had either worked for the company as consultants or received monies from the company. Many more politicians and officials take positions as consultants after they leave office. This is known as the 'revolving door' syndrome. Obviously, this raises the question of how even-handedly they can act whilst in office. Many business interests often have too close a relationship with the Independent Regulatory Commissions that are supposed to assess objectively their compliance with the various laws and regulations.

Clearly, then, while pressure groups offer a great deal to any democracy, they may also advance the interests of wealthy business groups above those of the majority population. The rise of Political Action Committees has also led to accusations that influence is for sale. Edward Kennedy spoke about the US legislature being 'the best Congress that money can buy' and others have written of a 'coin-operated Congress'.

e The candidate drops in one or two good US examples at the end, but this remains an overly theoretical response. This level of theoretical understanding would earn a grade B, but for higher marks, more of an attempt should have been made to link the discussion to the issue of excessive pressure group influence in the USA.

Question 8.2

How important are 'iron triangles' within the US system of government?

(15 minutes)

e 'Iron triangles' are dealt with in a number of textbooks. That said, this would probably be one of the more obscure questions you might face in the examination. As always with these shorter questions, you need to give a clear, precise definition early on and then try to make two or three developed points regarding importance. The phrase 'within the US system of government' allows you to look beyond the passage of legislation if you want to, though you could certainly produce an A-grade response focusing entirely on the importance of 'iron triangles' with regard to the legislative process.

■ ■ ■

A-grade answer to question 8.2

The term 'iron triangle' is applied to the close relationships that can develop between the key pressure group in a particular field, the appropriate congressional committee and the executive agency or bureau of the department with responsibility for the area. As such triangles are formed, other interested parties are excluded from the 'policy loop', to their detriment. The writer Richard L. Kolbe uses the example of a triangle concerning wheat production, but such relationships probably exist in most areas of policy. What makes these iron triangles so strong is that those involved are able to offer each other desirable benefits.

e The candidate gives a clear definition and touches on an example — this is exactly what is required here.

One such benefit is hinted at when commentators talk about the 'revolving door syndrome'. The 'revolving door syndrome' relates to the way in which individuals in Congress or in the executive often walk out of office into well-paid consultancy jobs with special interest groups and, at the same time, former consultants find themselves being offered key positions in the administration of the day. This mixing and moving of personnel within an iron triangle strengthens it further and makes it even more unlikely that an 'outsider' will be let into the loop. In the wake of the Enron scandal, for example, the *Guardian* reported that Robert Rubin (Clinton's treasury chief) had later become a senior figure at Enron creditors Citigroup and had lobbied the Bush administration on behalf of Enron. In cases such as this, there is always a danger of agency capture. This is said to have occurred when a special interest group is able to control the government agency that should be overseeing or regulating the area of policy with which the group is concerned. Once in such a position, the group can often exclude other interested parties from the administration of policy and short-circuit the regulatory process.

This answer, particularly the strong final paragraph, covers all three Assessment Objectives. The reference to the 'revolving door syndrome' and the example from the *Guardian* strengthen it further, securing a grade A.

■ ■ ■

Question 8.3

What is meant by the term 'soft money'?

(10 minutes)

 Any definition of 'soft money' will probably involve some mention of what 'hard money' is, even though the latter isn't mentioned in the question. A good answer will refer to the restrictions placed on 'hard money' by the Campaign Finance Act of 1974. This will allow you to define 'soft money' as contributions that fall outside the act's restrictions. You should have some idea of the purposes that this money can be put to according to the act (following its amendment in 1979). Top candidates might also refer to the 2002 Bipartisan Campaign Finance Reform Act. If allowed to stand, this should mark the end of 'soft money'.

■ ■ ■

A-grade answer to question 8.3

Amid accusations of corruption in the late 1960s and early 1970s, Congress passed the 1974 Federal Elections Campaign Act. This act placed limits on the amount of money that individuals and organisations could give to candidates directly — so-called 'hard money'. In 1979, however, in an effort to revive grass-roots politics, Congress passed an act allowing money to be collected and spent on measures aimed at increasing voter registration ('registration drives') and turnout ('get out the votes' programmes). This 'soft money' was not covered by the 1974 campaign finance limits and was normally given to the parties rather than the candidates themselves. By the 1980s, the line between this 'soft money' and the regulated 'hard money' was becoming blurred. A lot of the 'soft money' was effectively being spent on candidates' campaigns, through issue-advocacy for example. By 1992, this 'soft money' totalled over $250 million.

 The candidate provides a clear and accurate definition here, together with detail explaining the context. Even without the next paragraph this would be a high-scoring answer.

The Bipartisan Campaign Finance Reform Act of 2002 aimed, amongst other things, to close the 'soft money' loophole. The act amended the 1974 and 1979 regulations, effectively banning 'soft money' contributions to the national parties. Under the act, parties had to dispose of all such remaining funds by 31 December 2002. The act is currently facing a number of legal challenges.

 Only those candidates with a genuine interest in the subject — or enthusiastic teachers — would be able to provide such a clear assessment of the way in which the 2002 act could affect 'soft money'. This would certainly take what was already a very strong answer to the top of the mark range.

■ ■ ■

C-grade answer to question 8.3

'Soft money' is money that is given to political parties during elections, rather than directly to the candidates themselves. It was supposed to help parties organise the 'grass roots', but in recent years some of this money has been used more directly on the candidates' campaigns. This goes against what 'soft money' was supposed to be and has led some people to call for tighter regulations.

 This answer is along the right lines but it lacks the depth, breadth and precision of a higher-grade response. There is no mention of the law relating to campaign finance or to 'hard money'. Figures would be useful too, as would specific detail regarding how this 'soft money' is spent.

■ ■ ■

Question 8.4

Outline the role played by Political Action Committees within the US system.

(15 minutes)

 This question asks you to look at the role played by PACs, but you will need to explain what PACs are and where they came from early on in the essay, if not in your introduction. Most candidates should be able to name a PAC and recognise the central role that they play in the financing of presidential and congressional elections. Many textbooks provide detailed statistics on campaign finance, and using figures lends essays a degree of authority.

■ ■ ■

A-grade answer to question 8.4

Political Action Committees (PACs) are organisations that collect and channel money to candidates running for political office. The expansion in PACs took place following the campaign finance reform of the early 1970s, particularly after the 1974 Campaign Finance Act. This reform prevented unions, corporations and trade associations from making campaign contributions directly to candidates. PACs, therefore, became the middlemen, collecting together contributions from such groups as well as from other individuals and then channelling the monies towards the candidates who might best serve the interests of the PAC contributors.

> **e** The term 'Political Action Committee' is not easy to define, but the candidate makes a reasonable attempt here.

PACs have proliferated in recent years. There were only 600 in 1974, yet by 2000 the number had risen to 4,500. These groups contribute an enormous amount of money to candidates. In 2000, for example, the Realtors PAC (real estate agents) contributed a total of $3.5 million. In the same year the PAC working for the National Rifle Association raised nearly $18 million. Interestingly, 75% of all PAC money goes to incumbent candidates. Some see this as dangerous because it gives incumbents greater resources with which to defend their position. Good 'challengers' are therefore severely disadvantaged. According to a Harris poll in 2001, 83% of Americans believe that 'PACs have too much power and influence in Washington'.

> **e** **This level of factual recall can be difficult and the statistics provided here are more than would be expected in examination conditions. On the whole this is a good answer, but given the title, more of a focus on the role of PACs would have been beneficial.**

C-grade answer to question 8.4

Political Action Committees (PACs) have the role of channelling money to candidates in elections. By doing this, they hope to influence the outcome of elections because those candidates who are better funded are able to produce better election materials and buy up more television airtime.

PACs hope that, once elected, the candidates they have helped will return the favour by supporting policies that will benefit those who set up the PACs in question. It's a kind of 'you scratch my back and I'll scratch yours' arrangement.

The Enron scandal showed just how totally dodgy all of this is. According to the *Guardian*, 71 Senators and 188 House members had received campaign contributions from Enron and the company had spent $5.8 million on federal election campaigns over 12 years. Congressmen who take money from PACs face a conflict of interests because they must choose whether to represent their constituents' interests or those of their financial masters.

> **e** Some good general points are made here and the candidate shows a good awareness of the Enron scandal and how it relates to PACs and election finance. The answer could have been improved by demonstrating a clearer understanding of what PACs are and how they operate, and by adopting a more sophisticated style.

Comparative Government & Politics

Questions and Answers

This section of the guide covers a range of answers to the kind of examination questions that you will be faced with at the end of your A2 course. It is divided into eight topics — Topics 9–12 deal with comparative government and Topics 13–16 look at debates in comparative politics.

Each question has an indication of the amount of time that you might have in which to complete your answer. This is a guideline only — you should adjust these to the demands of the examination questions for your specification. The answers given here are not supposed to be perfect — each answer simply represents one way of approaching the question given and the grade that it might have achieved.

Examiner's comments

Examiner's comments are preceded by the icon [e]. Immediately after each question, before the student answer, there is an examiner's advice section which outlines the focus and scope of the question. Following each answer an examiner's comment (in bold) summarises the main strengths and weaknesses of the answer. Shorter examiner's comments are inserted throughout the answers too. Read all of these examiner's advice and comment sections carefully — they indicate what you need to do in order to get an A-grade mark for the question.

Constitutions

Question 9.1

Outline the difference between a 'federal system' and a 'unitary system'.

(15 minutes)

e You need to have a good theoretical understanding of the two types of system in order to get a good mark here. It is also important, however, to remember that this question is designed to test your study of UK and US constitutions. As a result, you also need to show an understanding of the federal nature of the US constitution (perhaps mentioning the 10th Amendment) and the unitary nature of the UK constitution (recognising the extent and the limitations of the devolution process).

A-grade answer to question 9.1

A federal system such as that of the USA divides power clearly between the central ('federal') government and the local regions or states. This division of power is normally set out formally in an entrenched constitution. This means that it is impossible for the central government to remove power from the individual states or to abolish them altogether. In the United States the constitution explicitly gives powers to the federal government, which are called the enumerated powers and include elements such as the power to declare war. The 10th Amendment states that any powers not granted to the federal government by the constitution are reserved to the individual states — unless these powers are explicitly denied to the states elsewhere in the document — or to the people. These are called the reserved powers and include decisions over, for example, the regulation of state education and whether or not to have the death penalty. In the US federal system, some powers are also shared between federal and state governments (e.g. the right to levy taxes).

In a unitary state, all power originates from the central government. In the UK this means that parliament is sovereign and local government only has the power to do what central government allows it to do. If a branch of local government does something not authorised by central government, it is acting ultra vires and may be subject to legal action. Parliament can delegate some of its powers to another tier of government (as through the recent devolution schemes) but this does not turn the UK into a federal state. This is because parliament can take back this power from local government at any time.

e **The candidate gives a clear definition, applied accurately in the US and UK context. The last two sentences are an excellent summary.**

C-grade answer to question 9.1

A federal system is one where different parts of the country have different rules. In the USA, the central or federal government has powers over some things (e.g. defence) but the individual states have control over other things. In over 30 states, for example, they still have the death penalty. Some states use lethal injection, some use the electric chair and some still allow hanging or firing squads, in theory. Different states also have different rules over things such as abortion. The Supreme Court has said that individual states cannot ban abortion totally, but many states have removed state funding for it or made it illegal to carry out abortions in state premises. Some states have even removed abortion techniques from the medical training given to surgeons. In the UK, things are different. We have a unitary state. This means that all of the power in London rests with the Westminster Parliament. As a result, we all have the same laws. For example, in the 1960s parliament legalised abortion over the whole country and abolished the death penalty throughout the whole country. This is the difference between a federal and a unitary system.

The candidate demonstrates a fair understanding of the terms and is able to give some accurate and relevant examples in support of the points made. However, far more could be done to show an appreciation of the theory behind these examples (e.g. the importance of the 10th Amendment). The answer should also make use of appropriate concepts and terminology (sovereignty, authority, enumerated, entrenched, reserved etc.).

Question 9.2

Examine the difficulty faced in achieving constitutional change in the USA as compared to that in the UK.

(20 minutes)

This question is phrased in a rather more straightforward fashion than question 1.1 because it specifies 'constitutional change' rather than 'political change'. This subtle difference should make for a more focused essay, which is important given the limited time available. You obviously need to have a good knowledge of the processes by which UK and US constitutions can be 'changed'. On the US side of your answer, at least, this might include the way in which the Supreme Court is said to have a quasi-legislative power through its role as interpreter of the constitution. Supreme Court judges can, in effect, 'change' the constitution, without changing its words.

A-grade answer to question 9.2

The constitution of the USA and the UK are different in many respects, not least because the US constitution is codified, whereas its UK equivalent remains something of a 'botch-up' drawn together from a number of different sources. Another key difference that is linked to this is the manner in which constitutional change can be achieved in either country.

> ℮ This is a clearly written and focused introduction. However, the use of slang, i.e. 'botch-up', should be avoided, even if the words are put in quotes as the candidate has done here.

The fact that the US constitution is codified often leads people to suggest that it is rigid rather than flexible. Whilst the amendment process is tortuous, however, the constitution is anything but rigid. Indeed, it has shown itself to be incredibly flexible and adaptable in the 214 years since it was framed. This flexibility has been provided not only by the possibility of amendment but also by the ability of the courts — ultimately the US Supreme Court — to interpret the document and apply it to each new age. The legality of practices never dreamt of when the constitution was written has been assessed through this process of interpretation and, at the same time, the Supreme Court has been able to update its own interpretations of the same constitutional passage over a period of time. In this sense the constitution is a truly living document.

There have only been 27 amendments in over 200 years and 10 of those were agreed together in 1791 as the Bill of Rights. The amendment procedure set out in Article V of the constitution allows for two clear stages. The first involves proposing a change and the second is its approval. Constitutional amendments can be formally proposed in one of two ways — either with a two-thirds majority in each chamber of Congress, or through a National Constitutional Convention called by at least two-thirds of states. The latter route has never been used. Once formally proposed, the amendment must be ratified, again in one of two ways — either by three-quarters of state legislatures voting to ratify the amendment (normally within a certain time) or by three-quarters of states calling State Constitutional Conventions and ratifying the proposed amendment (used only for the 21st Amendment).

> ℮ This section contains much sound material. It is perhaps a little too descriptive, but it is helpful to spell out the amendment process clearly at this stage.

As well as formally amending the words of the US constitution, the unique position of the US Supreme Court as interpreter of the constitution allows it to define what the words that are there actually mean at any given time. Thus, the court was able to rule that racial segregation was not unconstitutional in principle in *Plessey* v. *Ferguson* (1896), yet later argued that segregation always created inequality and was therefore illegal under the 14th amendment in *Brown* v. *Board of Education, Topeka* (1954). Though the words of relevant passages in the constitution had not been amended between the two cases, their meaning had been altered totally.

The situation in the UK is slightly different. The UK constitution remains uncodified, its most important source being parliamentary statute. These acts of parliament are, however, no different from any other acts of parliament in that they can just as easily be repealed. None of this statute is properly entrenched, as the US constitution is, and there is little to stop a government with a large majority in the Commons from making sweeping constitutional changes simply by passing a new statute or repealing existing ones. Thus, the whole structure of parliament was changed with the House of Lords Reform Bill and hand-guns were outlawed by statute just months after the Dunblane massacre. Neither of these constitutional changes could have been made quickly in the USA. Any fundamental reform of the Senate would require an amendment to Article 1 of the US constitution and any ban on hand-guns would require the removal or re-drafting of the 2nd Amendment. The courts in the UK are also in a far weaker position. Whereas the US Supreme Court can declare government acts or actions unconstitutional, striking them down, the UK courts can only act against government where the government or a minister has acted unlawfully. Even then, those governments found guilty of such lawless behaviour can simply pass an act through, closing the loophole retrospectively and wiping away the minister's 'crime'.

> It is always better to write comparatively throughout, rather than spending half of the answer on the USA and then half on the UK. That said, this candidate clearly has sound knowledge and understanding and easily does enough to meet the criteria for a grade A.

C-grade answer to question 9.2

In the USA the constitution can only be amended through a long, drawn-out process. This process is set out in Article V of the US constitution. In 26 out of the 27 times that the constitution has been amended, this process has involved passing a proposal through both the House and the Senate — with a two-thirds majority — before securing the approval of three-quarters of all states. This is quite difficult to do. Ten of these amendments were passed in 1791 and only 17 have been passed in the 212 years since. When you think of how much society has changed in that time, it is amazing that so few amendments have been made. This must be due to the fact that the process is so difficult rather than because more changes haven't been needed.

In the UK, the constitution has statute law as its main source. This is simply law passed by parliament. As a result, the most fundamental of constitutional changes can be made through the same process as is used to pass any law. This is why it was so easy for Blair's government to abolish all but 92 of the hereditary peerages, even though they hadn't really explained where reform of the Lords was going to end up. They just passed a law. Their attempt to abolish the role of Lord Chancellor — one of the oldest positions in government — simply by announcing a cabinet reshuffle was in a similar vein. Though this was eventually found to require statutory approval, this is easily achieved in the UK. In the USA, it would be far more difficult, if not impossible, to remove an office as important as this one.

 This answer is slightly stronger on the UK material than on the US, but it is reasonably focused and accurate. It is weak in terms of range and depth — for example, the candidate does not consider the role of the Supreme Court in effecting changes in the meaning of the US constitution. A greater willingness to use political vocabulary would also allow for more convincing analysis and evaluation.

Question 9.3

'The US constitution is entrenched and rigid; the UK has no constitution worthy of the name.' To what extent would you agree with this view?

(45 minutes)

It is important not to leave any of the assertions in the quotation unchallenged. Though we can accept, for example, that the US constitution is entrenched, some argue that it remains supremely flexible (rather than rigid) as a result of the US Supreme Court's role of interpreting the ageing document and applying it to each new age. We might take issue too with the rather damning appraisal of the UK constitution. It might be worthwhile, therefore, to set out some of the problems with the quotation in the introduction, before proceeding to outline the agenda for the discussion. Although it is always dangerous to conclude in the introduction, it is perfectly acceptable to point out that a large part of the quotation in question is open to debate.

A-grade answer to question 9.3

Most dictionaries define the term 'constitution' as having one of two meanings. The first is a clear and codified set of rules detailing the precise relationships between the various elements of government and between the government and the people. The second is a spirit or style of government — a system where the rules are not all written down in a single document but where everyone works within a combination of traditions and practices and various written statutes under the principles of reasonableness and the rule of law.

This is a good, direct introduction. If you disagree with part or all of what is said in a stimulus quotation, it is good practice to mention this early on.

Clearly, no one would argue that the UK has a constitution that would fit the first definition. It must, therefore, have a constitution of the second type — for no state can operate without some framework of rules, however disparate that set of rules might be. The USA fits more neatly into the first definition, though we should remember that the US constitution is not set in stone. Although its words change rarely — only 17 times in the 212 years since the ratification of the Bill of Rights — its meaning is adapted and moderated over time, not least through the work of the US Supreme Court.

The various articles of the US constitution provide a framework within which everyone in the USA — individuals and institutions — must operate. This framework is certainly 'entrenched and rigid' in the sense that the words of the constitution are extremely hard to change. A Constitutional Amendment most often requires a two-thirds majority in both the House and the Senate before it is confirmed by three-quarters of all states. The Founding Fathers put this tortuous mechanism in place because they wanted to ensure that the system they had spent so long finalising would not simply be changed on a whim. The result of this deep entrenchment is that even the most harmless of Constitutional Amendments have sometimes proven impossible to pass. The failed Equal Rights Amendment is an excellent example of how difficult it can be to make the kinds of changes that would simply be passed through the UK Parliament on a nod.

Though the words of the constitution are difficult to change, however, its meaning is not. Starting in 1803, the US Supreme Court has established the power of judicial review. In essence, this is the power to interpret the constitution when disputes arise over its meaning. In this way the court has been able to infer the meaning of the document when new problems have emerged (e.g. pornography on the internet) and effectively to change the meaning of the constitution in the light of changes in society and new research. In 1896, for example, the court ruled that blacks and whites could be separated on trains provided their accommodation was 'equal'. In 1954, however, it ruled that separation would always create inequality and, therefore, that segregation was wrong and should be ended. Thus, though the constitution is certainly entrenched, it is not necessarily rigid. Through the work of the Supreme Court it remains flexible and the judgements of the court — the legal precedents — are actually much the same as what we call case law in the UK.

The UK constitution, being uncodified, has its basis in a number of key sources. First there is statute law. In the absence of a codified and entrenched document, statute law — the laws passed by the UK Parliament — is supreme. This statute law is written down, but whereas the US constitution can fit on to 15 or so pages at the back of a school textbook, the various statutes make up a rather more bulky source. There are other sources of the UK constitution, too. Case law or common law, as mentioned previously, has a part to play in setting out the framework of rules. A lot of the original law concerning civil liberties and a good deal of consumer protection rests on common law. Traditions or conventions also play their part. The 'rule' that a government resigns following a lost vote of confidence is, for example, only a convention. There is no legal way of forcing it to do so. European laws also take precedence over UK law under the 1972 European Communities Act.

🄴 The candidate might have mentioned 'works of authority' too, though there is an issue of time here and it is probably better to keep the argument moving.

Although the UK constitution has various sources, parliament can overturn any of them simply by passing a regular statute. This makes the UK constitution very flexible but, at the same time, makes any elements of the political system and everyone's rights subject to the whims of the majority government. The recent reform of the House of Lords illustrates this problem. The government used its Commons majority and the ultimate threat of the Parliament Act to force through a first stage of reform before even working out what the second stage was going to be. Thus a government with a large majority was able to change a fundamental part of the system of government without having to make it over any hurdle more demanding than passing the measure through a House in which it had a 166-vote majority.

We can see that the US constitution, though firmly entrenched, is not rigid in the way that this entrenchment might lead us to expect. The UK constitution is worthy of the name 'constitution', but it is of a fundamentally different style and nature — being uncodified — than its US counterpart. The quotation in the title therefore does a disservice to both constitutions.

🄴 **This is clearly an A-grade response. The candidate tackles the question directly and addresses all of the points raised in the title. The balance between the US and the UK parts of the answer is good, though it would have been better to go for a more comparative structure and thereby avoid lengthy sections on each country.**

■ ■ ■

C-grade answer to question 9.3

A constitution is a body of rules that defines the way in which a state or society is organised. It sets out the way in which power is distributed between the government and the people, and between the government's various parts. By doing this, a constitution provides a framework upon which more complex rules, structures and processes can be built.

🄴 The essay starts with a clear definition.

There are two distinct styles of constitution. The first consists of a full and authoritative set of rules written down in a single place. Such constitutions are said to be codified — this describes the US constitution, for example. The second type is those which are less tangible because they have evolved over time from a variety of sources and are not written down in a single document. Such constitutions are referred to as uncodified, like the UK constitution.

The fact that the UK constitution is uncodified does not mean, however, that it is 'unwritten'. Some of its sources are in written form, including its most important source — statute law. Acts of parliament are referred to as statutes. Some of these statutes play a significant role in outlining the extent and distribution of government powers; the Parliament Acts of 1911 and 1949, for example, limit the power of the House of Lords. Other statutes outline our rights within a democracy; in the various Representation of the People Acts, for example, rules governing elections and the franchise are set out.

> This is all accurate detail, but an examiner might be concerned at the lack of comparative material.

The second main source of the UK constitution is common law. Common law consists of established customs and precedent developed through the actions of judges. This 'precedent' is often referred to as 'case law' or 'judge-made law'. When a case is heard, the court generally looks for previous examples of similar cases and seeks to follow precedent when arriving at a decision. Where no precedent exists, the decision made sets a precedent itself, though in areas such as this it is common for the case to be passed up through the appeals process before a final judgement is made.

The third key source of the constitution is convention. Conventions are traditions or customs that have evolved over time and have, through deference to precedent, become accepted rules of behaviour. Unlike common law, however, conventions will not stand up in a court of law. Important conventions include the doctrines of individual and collective ministerial responsibility.

The fourth source of the constitution is European Union law and treaties. The increasing globalisation of politics and UK involvement in supranational organisations have led some to question the extent to which statute law is still the overriding source of our constitution. UK membership of the EU is particularly significant in this respect. In passing the 1972 European Communities Act, European law and regulations were given precedence over national laws. Thus, it is argued, statute law no longer conquers all and parliament is no longer sovereign.

The final source of the UK constitution is works of authority. Over time, some of these books have themselves become part of the constitutional framework because they codify practices not outlined on paper elsewhere. Erskine May's *Parliamentary Practice* and A. V. Dicey's *Introduction to the Study of the Law of the Constitution* are the best-known examples.

In the USA the constitution is easier to identify because it is all in one document (i.e. codified). The US constitution is sovereign and all other laws, conventions etc. are subject to it. The only other thing that might be considered a source of constitutional law could be the interpretations of the constitution made by the Supreme Court. This is a bit like case law in the UK. Because the court decides what the words of the constitution mean, its judgements actually become a bit like part of the constitution.

So the title is wrong to say that the UK has no constitution, but the US constitution is obviously easier to get hold of and understand.

❷ **This is a fairly solid, if a rather pre-learnt and descriptive, response. The main problem here is that the answer is not sufficiently comparative. A single paragraph on the USA, tagged on to the end of the essay, is not enough to achieve a top grade.**

Legislatures

Question 10.1

How effectively can the legislature and the executive control each other's actions in the UK and the USA?

(45 minutes)

 This title asks you to examine the nature of the relationships between the executives and the legislatures in each country in question. Terms such as separation of powers, checks and balances, accountability and scrutiny will therefore be crucial. The title does not present an obvious way of structuring an answer, but a good idea might be to look at a series of different aspects of power or policy (e.g. domestic policy, foreign policy, appointments, control of finance) and then to look at how the executives and legislatures of each country interact within each area. The student answer given below is less structured than it could be, but it scores highly in other areas.

A-grade answer to question 10.1

The relationship between the legislative and executive branches in the UK and the USA is very interesting. As separation of powers is incomplete in Britain, the executive has substantial power. While the UK is said to have 'parliamentary sovereignty', the phrase 'government sovereignty' may be more accurate.

 The candidate makes some good points here, although the paragraph could have been structured better.

One vital way in which the executive can control legislators' actions is through the whipping system. The chief whip and Lord Commissioners (assistant whips) are members of the government. They keep a voting record and can apply pressure to dissenting members of their party. In extreme cases, as happened in John Major's period of office, the party whip (membership) may be removed. Although government whips only have authority over government party members, the government has the majority of seats in the Commons and so can still push through legislation.

In contrast, the American president cannot exert pressure using whipping. Whipping is an internal congressional party matter. It has been said that 'the only power the president has is the power to persuade'. When influencing legislators, this is true. Johnson used to telephone Congressmen in the middle of the night to pressurise them. Congressional whips have little power beyond curtailing floor access.

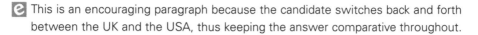

 This is an encouraging paragraph because the candidate switches back and forth between the UK and the USA, thus keeping the answer comparative throughout.

As the UK executive sits in parliament, cabinet members can exert direct pressure in the chambers, through speeches and rhetoric. The American executive must find sympathetic Congressmen to argue for legislation on its behalf.

As the executive sits in parliament, and relies on its majority to maintain authority, parliament can destroy the executive. Governments with small majorities, like Major's, can be sabotaged by a small group of government legislators — Major's 'bastards'. They can bring down the government with a 'vote of no confidence'.

In the USA, Congress does not enjoy this power, but it can impeach the president. The House of Representatives draws up charges and a trial follows in the Senate. This is a very significant curb on the executive actions.

As well as impeaching the president, Congress has the power to refuse to ratify presidential appointments. George Bush Senior's choice of Defense Secretary was refused after harassment allegations, while it took Reagan three attempts to replace a Supreme Court justice. Parliament has no such power over prime ministerial appointees.

Parliament can prevent a planned executive action by voting against a bill. The recent Security and Terrorism Bill had to be amended because of criticisms from MPs, including government backbenchers, that it was too draconian and extreme. Recent plans in a Criminal Justice Bill to scrap universal availability to jury trial have had to be reversed. Therefore parliamentary pressure can have a substantial influence on the executive.

Through whipping, the UK government can thwart a bill it dislikes. Similarly, the president can veto congressional legislation. However, the veto can be overturned by a two-thirds congressional majority. The 1978 Comprehensive Anti-Apartheid Act is a good example of this — it was passed despite a presidential veto.

Legislative committees are an essential way in which the legislature can control executive actions — by amending or dismissing proposed executive legislation and departments.

UK select committees scrutinise government departments, while standing committees scrutinise legislation. Standing committees are essential in controlling the executive. However, UK strict party discipline and lack of separation of powers allow the executive to dominate committees. Membership is in proportion to that of the House of Commons — so the government party has an automatic majority. In addition, Tony Banks recently commented on *Westminster Live* that 'even speaking in committee is seen as a disciplinary offence'. This shows how keen UK governments are to 'steam roll' through legislation. Committees often 'kangaroo' over entire sections, criticism of which led to the government's abortive attempt to remove Gwyneth Dunwoody as head of the Transport Select Committee.

Unlike the weak committees of parliament, congressional committees can tackle executive legislation properly. Chairs are very powerful and have substantial control over the passage of legislation. About 95% of bills 'die in committee'.

Another way in which committees can control the executive in America is funding. The Appropriations Committees — Ways and Means Committee in the House and Finance Committee in the Senate — allocate funding to executive departments, agencies and programmes. The Impoundment Act says that presidents must spend allocated funds within 45 days. This was brought about because of Nixon, who criticised piecemeal budgetary analysis and said that committees were allocating too much, increasing the federal budget deficit and raising inflation.

British select committees do not have as much power, nor can they question the budget to such an extent.

Both the Senate and the Lords are more outspoken and rebellious.

US separation of powers, through formal veto and override systems, gives distinct controlling powers (checks and balances) to executive and legislature.

The answer is falling apart a little here. The points being made are valid but the candidate — no doubt under time pressure — is unable to develop these points further.

In the UK, lack of separation, government domination and strict party discipline mean that the executive has unhindered control over committees and votes. Of course, in the USA Congress and the president can be of opposite parties, causing 'gridlock'. However, party is a much more influential feature in the UK. The UK Parliament has weak powers of control in relation to Congress.

This is an A-grade response, though not at the top of the level. It covers AO1 well, but the argument could have been better structured, particularly towards the end.

Question 10.2

How effectively do the upper chambers in the US and UK systems (Senate and Lords) discharge their duties?

(45 minutes)

Before considering the effectiveness of each chamber, you need to identify precisely what 'duties' the Senate and the Lords have. Whereas the Senate's 'duties' are fairly easy to pin down, due to the codified nature of the US constitution, the Lords is in such a state of flux at present that it might be difficult to obtain up-to-date infor-

mation regarding where the House is 'going'. In situations such as this, examiners do not expect you to be absolutely up-to-the-minute on every aspect of Lords reform. They do, however, expect you to be able to identify a range of duties common to virtually all legislative chambers (e.g. debate, forming legislation, scrutiny of the executive) and then to assess the extent to which the Senate and the Lords discharge such duties today.

B-grade answer to question 10.2

Although the Lords and the Senate are seen as being the upper chambers within their own legislatures, it is difficult to compare them because this is one of the only things that they have in common. The two chambers are vastly different in terms of composition, role and power.

Whereas the Senate is made up of 100 Senators, the House of Lords currently consists of around 700 peers. Senators serve a fixed 6-year term. Since the reforms of 1998, most of the Lords hold their positions for life, or at least until the reform of the Lords is complete. Finally, the Senate is an elected chamber, whereas the Lords is largely appointed, with a rump of 92 converted hereditary peers.

The differences in the composition of the two chambers have a significant impact on their roles. As a directly elected chamber (since the 17th Amendment?), the Senate can reasonably claim to have legitimacy and an electoral mandate. This means that the Senate has as much right to legislate as the other chamber in Congress — the House of Representatives. This much is clear from the US constitution, which states that they hold equal power over legislation. The Lords, in contrast, is an unelected chamber. This means that it must naturally defer to the elected chamber — the Commons — because the Commons has an electoral mandate and can be held accountable by the voters. The Salisbury Convention states that the Lords should not reject a bill at second reading where it was part of the manifesto on which the government was elected. The Parliament Acts of 1911 and 1949 have also limited the power of the Lords to delay legislation to 1 year (1 month for money bills).

The candidate demonstrates an excellent level of knowledge and understanding here, though it is better not to question your own facts even if you are unsure about them.

In legislation, then, the Lords clearly has far less power than the Senate. The Senate has the ability to kill or amend legislation at will. Where it passes a different version of a bill to that passed in the House, a conference committee looks to reconcile the two versions. No bill can be passed without the approval of the Senate. The Lords, in contrast, can inconvenience the government by delaying a bill, but cannot ultimately kill it. Having said this, the threat of delay is often enough to persuade the government to make concessions in the form of amendments.

Both the Senate and the Lords have a role as great debating chambers. The fact that there are so few Senators (as opposed to House members) means that debates are often informed and considered. The privilege of speaking without interruption in the Senate has developed into the power to filibuster. The Lords is also a respected debating chamber. Many of those in the Lords are experienced or knowledgeable in a particular area and this leads to a very high quality of debate. In the House of Representatives and the Commons things often appear rushed and ill thought through in comparison.

Both the Senate and the Lords have a judicial input — for the moment at least. The Senate hears all impeachment trials and can also reject the president's nominations to the US Supreme Court. Though the Lords has no such check on the prime minister's power of patronage, the Lords has traditionally been presided over by the head of the judiciary (the Lord Chancellor) and has included the judges who make up the highest national court of appeal — the Law Lords.

The Senate and the Lords also have foreign policy roles. The Lords takes the responsibility for scrutinising EU legislation in committee. The Senate has the role of confirming treaties negotiated by the president (by two-thirds).

These are the ways in which the Senate and the Lords differ and are similar.

🄴 **This answer is not long, but it is focused on the question. The essay is structured in a genuinely comparative fashion throughout. The candidate could, however, have given some actual examples in support of the theory.**

Question 10.3

Compare and contrast the roles and powers of parliamentary committees with their counterparts in Congress.

(45 minutes)

🄴 Structuring this essay is made easier by the fact that the UK and the USA have committees bearing the same names — standing committees and select committees. Better still, although they share the same names they are very different in nature, role, powers and effectiveness. This means that there are plenty of excellent opportunities for comparisons and contrasts. This is an essay that you should only attempt if you have revised legislative committees thoroughly.

A-grade answer to question 10.3

Committees play a crucial role in both the UK Parliament and the US Congress. In both countries, committees have a role in discussing and fine-tuning legislation. They can add amendments to bills, either to correct faults in the original bill or to extend the scope of the bill beyond its original remit. Committees also play a role in scrutinising the executive in both countries, not only by checking legislative proposals but also by keeping an eye out for inefficiencies and impropriety. Having said all of this, it is important to remember that the committees in the UK legislature are fundamentally different from those in the USA in a number of ways.

> e This is a perfectly adequate introduction. It could do more to set some kind of agenda for the discussion to come, but it does, at least, focus on the work of committees.

Committees in parliament broadly divide into two types — standing committees and select committees. Standing committees are ad hoc, being formed for the purpose of considering a piece of legislation. They are made up of between 15 and 60 members, the numbers from each party reflecting the composition of the House itself. Standing committees can sit for several months, suggesting minor changes and more serious amendments before 'reporting out' to the House. Select committees, in contrast, are not often as involved in the passage of legislation. Since 1979, departmental select committees have had the role of scrutinising the work of the various government departments. Not all select committees are, however, attached to a department. Of the non-departmental select committees, the Public Accounts Committee is one of the most high-profile and has the role of ensuring value for money in government. This committee has developed a fearsome reputation for making departments accountable for their spending.

Congressional committees are set up on a slightly different basis. Though standing committees exist in the House and the Senate, they are different in nature from their UK counterparts. First, US standing committees are permanent. Members of these committees often remain on the same committee for years, even decades. This means that they develop a real feel for their area. Second, US standing committees take on some of the role played by departmental select committees in the UK — that is, scrutinising the work of their executive department. US select committees are, therefore, different from UK departmental select committees. A select or special committee may be formed on an ad hoc basis to deal with an issue where investigations fall outside the normal scope of an existing standing committee or are likely to be on such a large scale as to affect the committee's normal work. A good example is the joint select committee on the Iran–Contra affair.

> e These two paragraphs are quite descriptive but are factually accurate and do address the question.

The real differences between UK and US committees, however, appear when you look at the way in which the committees work. In the USA, committees have enormous power. Committees and in particular their chairmen have the power to pigeonhole bills — effectively killing them. It is hard to imagine a situation in which a standing committee in the House of Commons would consider killing a government bill. This is partly because of the fact that party ties are so much stronger in the UK Parliament than they are in the US Congress. In the UK, the power of the whips does not stop at the committee door. In the USA, it is hard to see the influence of the whips anywhere, even on the floor of the House. In addition, specific committees, such as the House Rules Committee, have a power that is unique within the US system and unheard of in the UK. The House Rules Committee has the power to timetable and classify bills for House action once they have been reported out of committee. In the UK, it is the leader of the Commons who takes on much of this role and he or she is a cabinet member. By opening up bills to unlimited amendment or forcing the bill through unchanged (what would be called a guillotine in the UK), the Rules Committee has the power of life or death over all important bills.

> This is a more analytical paragraph. It also includes a number of quite sophisticated points (e.g. on the role of party whips within committees).

US committees work in a totally different way from their UK counterparts. US standing committees hold detailed hearings in which they can force witnesses to come forward to give evidence. This is not a power that UK committees have. US committees also have access to far greater resources. Congress has over 30,000 permanent staff and this means that US committees can conduct detailed research on the merits of a piece of legislation. In the UK, committee resources are far more modest.

Committee chairmen are also of crucial importance in the USA. The president cannot control who takes the chair in key committees. Congress is its own master in this area, an aspect of the separation of powers. The prime minister in the UK can normally use the whips to ensure that sympathetic party members are in control of all of the key committees, whereas in the USA the president cannot even be sure that his or her own party is going to control the legislature. Committee chairmen and women are often fiercely independent in the USA.

In conclusion, though we can see that the committee systems in each country appear to have obvious similarities, they are fundamentally different. It has been said that 'Congress in session is Congress on show' whereas 'Congress in committee is Congress at work' and I agree with this view. Compared to these US congressional committees, parliamentary committees rarely cause the majority party in the Commons any sleepless nights.

> **This candidate demonstrates a good level of knowledge and understanding. Though the answer could have been better structured and have a clearer sense of direction, this response would place it in the A-grade band.**

Executives

Question 11.1

Which has the greater influence over the detail and direction of government policy, the federal bureaucracy in the USA or the civil service in the UK?

(45 minutes)

🄴 Though most students would feel confident dealing with a question on the UK civil service, few ever take on questions involving the federal bureaucracy, however straightforward. In a recent examination, only around 15 out of a sample of 300 students opted for a question similar to this one. The other 285 opted for one of the other two questions available on the paper — even though they were both much more difficult in some respects. In order to feel confident when answering this question, you need to have a clear idea of what the federal bureaucracy is. What does it consist of? Which parts of the executive are in it and which are not? Unless you can answer these questions, you should not even consider tackling this type of title.

■ ■ ■

A/B-grade answer to question 11.1

The US federal bureaucracy and the UK civil service are the unelected administrative parts of their respective governments. Before we can assess their policy influence, however, we must identify precisely what each 'body' consists of.

🄴 This is rather a brief paragraph, but there is no harm in deploying this kind of introduction and getting straight into the main part of the essay — particularly if you are pushed for time or if you struggle to write a great deal in timed conditions.

The federal bureaucracy employs some 3,000 staff, working throughout the country in federal offices. Many of those staff work for one of the executive departments but others work within executive agencies or independent regulatory commissions. There are currently 14 executive departments, each headed by a member of the Bush cabinet, for example Rod Paige, who heads up education. Technically, at least, the US cabinet could itself be considered part of the federal bureaucracy because its members are unelected administrators.

In addition to the executive departments, there are a number of independent executive agencies (IEAs). These agencies were set up to provide a greater degree of focus and control in specific areas of policy. They act independently of executive departments and are funded separately, making their budget requests direct to the Office of Management and Budget. Prominent IEAs include the Environmental Protection Agency (EPA) and the Central Intelligence Agency (CIA). Agencies are normally headed by an individual ('director') who directs their efforts. The EPA, for example, is headed by Christie Todd Whitman.

Alongside the departments and the IEAs there are the independent regulatory commissions (IRCs). Congress passes acts which set up regulatory commissions in many areas of industrial and commercial life. Naturally, as the federal government has expanded, this role has become more significant. Each commission is headed by a board that averages five members, each of whom has been appointed by a president for a fixed length of time. One good example of an IRC is the Federal Reserve Board (controlling aspects of monetary policy); another is the Civil Aeronautics Board (licensing and regulating airlines).

All of this knowledge is commendable, but the approach is in danger of being too descriptive. As you write, keep asking yourself, 'Am I answering the question here or simply telling the examiner everything that I know about this topic?'

The UK civil service also consists of a number of different bodies, its total staff numbering around 400,000. In reality, however, only 4,000 or so top civil servants in the administration group might have a significant influence over policy. Traditionally, the UK civil service was said to be based on three key principles: anonymity, permanence and neutrality. However, civil servants, especially the top 1,000, are increasingly being pushed beyond this traditional role into a position where they are significantly more politicised. In some cases, civil servants are even called before the press — as though they and not the minister have responsibility for departmental policy and procedure. In the USA too, the civil service has become increasingly politicised at the top.

The rise of so-called 'special advisers' on both sides of the Atlantic has been a key feature of politics in the last 15 years. These special advisers often now appear to be answerable for policy. Some civil servants become publicly known and are, in some cases, identified as being responsible for the execution of policy (consider the Hutton Inquiry and the way in which the director of the Child Support Agency faced severe and public criticism over the agency's teething problems). Clearly, these top advisers may well have excessive influence. The rise of Alastair Campbell in the UK, for example, and the way in which George W. Bush has surrounded himself with what one insider called the 'crazy crew' that were marginalised even during his father's presidency, illustrate the changes taking place.

The 'crazy crew' point is a nice touch and reflects the fact that the candidate is clearly interested and aware of developments in US politics beyond the textbook.

While these top advisers and bureaucrats are important, we should not forget the many ways in which regular US and UK civil servants can manipulate, steer and obstruct the work of elected politicians. First, civil servants control information (and can either deny ministers essential information or drown the minister in paperwork). At the same time, ministers are often too busy with other engagements to keep a close eye on the work of their top bureaucrats. Even a competent minister can be hindered by the fact that top civil servants outnumber ministers ten to one in the UK. The 535 US Congressmen (House plus Senate) have a staff of 30,000. Civil servants also have other obvious advantages. In the UK top civil servants tend to stay in the department a lot longer than the ministers do. Ministers move between departments, on average, every 2 years or so. In the USA, cabinet members often stay in their jobs for far longer than elected politicians do. This helps them to network with other members of their department. Indeed, on both sides of the Atlantic ministers can go 'native' (becoming surrounded by the civil service and cut off from the reality outside their departments).

There is some excellent content here but the response is a little too descriptive. All of this factual content could be used far more productively within an analytical framework. This answer would fall on the borderline between grades A and B.

Question 11.2

'Neither the US cabinet nor its UK counterpart has much basis in law, yet they both exert a massive influence on the direction of policy in their respective countries.' How accurate is this view?

(45 minutes)

This is a nice question because the assessment given divides up neatly into two clear propositions and because both of these propositions allow for debate. The cabinet is not mentioned in the US constitution and in the UK much of what the cabinet does has its basis in convention, rather than law. As a result, the first proposition can largely be accepted. The second proposition is the more contentious one because few have ever seen the US cabinet as a body that exerts 'massive influence'. Indeed, most commentators have concluded that the US cabinet has little or no influence. At the same time, the UK cabinet, once seen as a central part of the decision-making machinery, is now often regarded as something of an irrelevance, both by those who have served on it (e.g. Mo Mowlam) and by those who study it. Though this judgement is probably a little harsh, it might be closer to the truth than the assessment in the title.

A-grade answer to question 11.2

In the time available, it is probably best to deal with this statement in two parts: first, that the US and UK cabinets have little basis in law; and second, that both cabinets exert a 'massive influence' over policy.

> **e** This is a rather functional introduction. It would be awarded no marks for style, but it does at least get the essay moving with direction and purpose.

To begin with the first part, the US constitution does not mention the cabinet by name. Though it assigns the role of chief executive to the president, the constitution leaves the structure of this executive, including the role and even the very existence of the cabinet, very much up in the air. The UK is faced with a similar situation. The fact that the UK has an uncodified constitution means that there is no formal and authoritative judgement on what the roles and/or powers of the UK cabinet are. In both countries, therefore, the role of cabinet has emerged by necessity as a result of convention.

We can now move on to the issue of whether or not both cabinets exert a 'massive influence' on policy. The US cabinet is different from its UK counterpart in the sense that its members do not sit simultaneously in the country's legislature. This is due to the separation of powers. No one person can hold office in more than one branch of the federal government. The US cabinet is also different from that in the UK because cabinet members are often specialists in their field — to the extent that it is not totally unheard of to see members holding their positions even after the transition from a Democrat chief executive to a Republican one. They are also free from the burden of re-election (not being elected legislators). As such, they can do what they think is right without having to worry too much about it. The only person who is likely to try to remove them is the president, and even this is relatively unlikely.

The scale of work undertaken by the US cabinet normally means that individual members work fairly independently of one another. The president is easily able to divide and rule, and the fact that the various secretaries compete for the president's attention tends to make the cabinet, as Richard Fenno noted, 'a schizophrenic body'. Cabinet meetings are still important, however, because they give members a chance to see one other and a chance to see the president. They also allow for the collection and dissemination of information and facilitate the resolution of interdepartmental conflicts, thereby focusing the collective effort. Despite these apparently important roles, the US cabinet has been seen as little more than a talking-shop for most of the time since its emergence. In recent months, however, some US cabinet members have become more actively and visibly involved in real debates and real decision-making processes, particularly over Iraq. Colin Powell (said to be the leading 'dove' in the administration) has been at odds with Donald Rumsfeld (a leading 'hawk') on a number of occasions. This suggests that the US cabinet plays a more meaningful role in the decision-making process than was thought previously. Ultimately, we might conclude, the extent to which a president makes use of his cabinet is largely down to the way in which he wants to use it. Some presidents have used cabinet on an almost weekly basis (e.g. Eisenhower) whereas others have scarcely called any cabinet meetings at all (e.g. Kennedy).

This is an excellent paragraph. The candidate makes some perceptive theoretical points and backs them up with appropriate, up-to-date examples. The level of awareness, particularly with regard to the US cabinet divisions over Iraq, is very pleasing.

In the UK the cabinet is different from its US counterpart in a number of respects. First, UK cabinet members are MPs. This means that they may well have a certain mandate or public profile that is separate and distinct from that of the prime minister or the cabinet as a whole. Gordon Brown, for example, probably has to be treated with a good deal more respect than most US cabinet members, because he has a natural constituency on the backbenches and has the potential to cause problems for Blair if he were forced out of government. Another difference is that UK cabinet members are more likely to be generalists than specialists and they move between departments, on average, once every 2 years. This means that they have little opportunity to specialise in a particular area and makes it difficult for them to have a large personal impact on the detail of policy. They probably have to rely on their departmental civil servants for the ideas, or at least the detail. The fact that UK cabinet members are appointed by the PM without any need for approval and that they are not subject to any fixed-term contract leaves the PM in a strong position. It is still seen as a big issue for the PM to sack more than one key heavyweight cabinet member in a day, whereas it probably wouldn't look as bad if the president did it in the US cabinet. The power to hire and fire ensures that all but the most rebellious cabinet members stay in check. The PM can also 'divide and rule' by using bilateral meetings, as Blair has done. This shows us that the UK cabinet has become more like its US counterpart because the PM is now able to dominate proceedings and marginalise rivals.

Neither the UK nor the US cabinet has much basis in law. This much is clear. The question of their influence over the direction of policy is more difficult to answer because it depends on the amount of influence that the US president or the UK prime minister is prepared to give them. In both countries this depends on factors such as the leadership style of the chief executive and the political context in which the leader has to operate.

This is a top A-grade answer. Though its structure could have been improved, the depth and range of examples and the manner in which the candidate has brought the various threads of the discussion together in the conclusion are impressive.

> ## Question 11.3
>
> 'Though the president is often seen as the most powerful man on Earth, due to America's global role, any president would envy the degree of control that the prime minister has in the UK system.' To what extent would you accept this judgement?
>
> (45 minutes)

 Most candidates choose questions comparing the US president and the UK prime minister in preference to others on an exam paper. This variation is fairly straight-forward but you should note the phrase 'envy the degree of control that the prime minister has in the UK system'. What the question is getting at, therefore, is not whether the PM or the president is the more powerful but whether the PM has more freedom within the UK system than the president has within the US system of government. This requires a discussion of constitutional devices such as the separation of powers and checks and balances, as well as a more traditional outline and comparison of powers.

■ ■ ■

A-grade answer to question 11.3

It is certainly true that the modern US president is widely regarded as being the most powerful man on Earth. We should not, however, see this as a totally new phenomenon. In the 1980s, the Speaker of the House, Thomas 'Tip' O'Neill, was heard to remark that 'the power of the presidency is awesome' and even before that, in the early 1970s, Arthur Schlesinger wrote of the rise of an 'Imperial Presidency'. Alongside the US president, the UK prime minister is always likely to end up looking rather less impressive, but this is not really the point that the quotation in the title is making. It suggests that, within the UK's systems and structures, the prime minister has a greater freedom of movement than his or her US counterpart. Is this true and, if so, why?

 This is an outstanding introduction. Although it does not explicitly set out an agenda for the essay that follows, this paragraph gets right to the heart of the question in the final two sentences.

The powers of the president are outlined clearly in the US constitution, as are the limitations on them. If we were to take the various articles of the constitution literally, then there would be very little that the president could do without the cooperation of at least one other branch of government. An example might be the passage of legislation. The constitution vests all legislative power in the hands of Congress. Though the president is given the rights to make a State of the Union Address and to veto bills in their entirety within a fixed time, Congress clearly has a lot more freedom from the executive than the UK Parliament does. Ultimately, Congress can pass a law without the approval of the president, by overriding a presidential veto. The president cannot even introduce a bill into Congress without help from friends on Capitol Hill.

In foreign policy too, the constitution ties the president's hands firmly. Though he is notionally commander-in-chief of the armed forces, it is Congress that retains the power to declare war. Though the president can negotiate treaties on behalf of the USA, his treaties must be ratified by two-thirds of the Senate — a very high hurdle (witness the Senate's rejection of Carter's SALT II Treaty). Presidential appointments are also made only on the majority approval of the Senate. Constitutionally, therefore, the president is clearly tied down in those few significant areas that we have had time to look at here. The fact that the president often faces a Congress dominated by a party other than the president's own only emphasises these checks on his freedom of movement.

In contrast, the UK prime minister appears more able to act independently of others. In exercising the monarch's prerogative powers, the prime minister can legally take the kinds of decisions that might require approval from another branch in the USA. The PM can wage war and sign treaties without parliamentary approval, though such decisions are normally run through parliament in order to garner legitimacy. When John Major signed the Maastricht Treaty in the early 1990s, his legal team assured him that, if it came to it, he did not need to get the treaty approved by parliament because he was signing it on behalf of the monarch. As Major recognised, however, it would probably be a cause for resignation were parliament formally to reject a treaty negotiated and signed by the PM. A number of US presidents, in contrast, have had to face this very humiliation.

> e A major strength of this section is that the candidate constantly links the discussion of the prime minister back to the points made earlier regarding the US president. This is a good way of keeping the comparative element of the answer at the forefront.

In domestic policy, too, the PM appears to be in a stronger position. The PM is able to sit in the legislature, along with his or her 100 or so government members, cabinet and party — which will, most likely, have a large majority in the Commons. This fusion of executive and legislative power and the tradition of majority government means that the PM and the cabinet can dominate the legislative timetable in a manner that would make any president 'envious'. Few government bills are ever amended significantly in the UK, let alone rejected. Compare that to the situation in the USA, where presidential projects routinely sink in a mountain of 'pork'. Even when presidents are in the fortunate position of having their own party in control of Congress, they cannot be sure of success. Indeed, some have suggested that 'gridlock' is just as common without divided government as it is with it. Clinton found this in 1993, when the Democrat-controlled Congress rejected his health reform plan.

It would, of course, be naive to think that the president's powers are routinely limited in the manner set out in the constitution. In times of national emergency, capable presidents have always been able either to outmanoeuvre Congress or shame it into submission by 'wrapping themselves in the flag'. Schlesinger was finishing his book *The Imperial Presidency* at the time that the Watergate scandal was breaking. The then president, Richard Nixon, later remarked that 'when the president does it, that means that it is not illegal', and this comment is a fair reflection of the condition of the presidency in the mid-1970s, before Congress reasserted itself. Some feel that we have arrived at the same point again, with Bush apparently free to act at will, under the cover of the 'war on terror'. Few people are prepared to criticise him openly in the wake of the events of 11 September 2001, though leading Democrats in Congress appear to be coming round to the idea that it might be time to take the gloves off again. In Britain too, commentators are increasingly referring to a 'presidential' Blair, who disregards his cabinet and rides roughshod over parliament and parliamentary traditions.

Clearly, due to the uncodified nature of the UK constitution, neither the extent of prime ministerial power nor the checks operating on it are likely to be easy to isolate. It is probably true to say that the PM can exercise his powers with a greater degree of freedom, at face value at least, but we should remember that the PM is only really exercising the monarch's prerogative powers. The president, in contrast, faces a range of constitutional checks, but these are often interpreted loosely where a national emergency demands speedy action. After all, in the modern age it is not always appropriate to debate your planned actions publicly through two chambers totalling 535 members.

e **The conclusion maintains the same high standard set by the introduction and which has been sustained throughout. This essay is hard to fault and would be awarded a high grade A.**

Judiciaries

Question 12.1

Explain what is meant by the term 'judicial independence'.

(10 minutes)

It is important to remember that judicial independence and judicial impartiality are not the same thing. The term 'judicial impartiality' relates to the idea that the judiciary should approach cases fairly, on their merits rather than from a position of personal bias. Judicial independence, on the other hand, relates to the idea that the judiciary, once appointed, should have the freedom to act in accordance with its view of the law, without outside interference or control. Though a lack of judicial independence may, therefore, lead to a lack of judicial impartiality, the two terms are not interchangeable. Make sure that you are defining the correct term.

A-grade answer to question 12.1

The term 'judicial independence' refers to the idea that the judiciary should be able to apply the law without interference from government. This principle is important because members of the public need to be able to feel confident that their cases are dealt with fairly, rather than on the whim of individual politicians who might have their own agenda or motives.

In the United States, the notion of judicial independence is helped by the appointment process, during which the president's choices must be approved by a Senate that is often controlled by another party. The fact that the US Supreme Court justices are appointed for life and can only be removed through the impeachment process also allows the justices to make their decision on the basis of the law rather than having to worry about their careers. No US Supreme Court justice has ever been removed through the impeachment process.

In the UK the position of Lord Chancellor has, historically, straddled the executive, the legislature and the judiciary. Some feel that this makes the appointment of top judges open to political influence. The government's commitment to abolishing the position and setting up an independent appointment commission for judges will help in this respect.

This is a model answer. The definition of the term is clear and concise and the candidate makes use of appropriate examples from the UK and the USA in highlighting some factors that might enhance or limit judicial independence.

D-grade answer to question 12.1

Judicial independence is where the judges make their decisions on the basis of the law rather than letting other factors influence them. Sometimes, judges have their own personal views on a particular issue and they might be tempted to do what they think, rather than what the law says. Judicial independence is where they put their own personal feelings to one side and do the right thing.

One thing that would make the judges less biased would be if they were appointed independently. This would make it less likely that judges would feel that they had to please the politicians who appointed them. In both the USA and the UK, leading politicians appoint top judges, so this means that there isn't very much judicial independence.

e **This is a weak answer because the candidate does not really demonstrate a good understanding of the term in question. A large part of the answer, in fact, talks about judicial impartiality rather than judicial independence. When the candidate does move on to more relevant areas the comments lack precision.**

Question 12.2

To what extent would you agree with the view that the US judiciary's power far exceeds that of the UK judiciary?

(45 minutes)

e Although you could adopt a number of equally valid and effective approaches in answering this question, there are several key differences that should be central to your answer. First, there is the question of sovereignty in each country. In the USA the constitution is, to all intents and purposes, sovereign. In the UK, however, parliament is said to be sovereign and statute law is supreme. This fact leads on directly to the second key point, which is that judicial review is fundamentally different in the USA and in the UK. In the USA, because the constitution is sovereign, the Supreme Court has the power to review other inferior laws and the actions of government against it. This means that it can declare unconstitutional and strike down any law or action that goes against the constitution through the process of judicial review. In the UK, in contrast, the courts can only declare the actions of government unlawful (*ultra vires*) where it has acted beyond the powers given to it in the statute in question. The UK courts cannot declare a statute unconstitutional because, in passing the act, parliament has made it constitutional — statute law being the highest source of the UK constitution. Understanding these two key points is the key to producing a good answer to this question.

A-grade answer to question 12.2

It is difficult to assess the relative power of the US and UK judiciaries without going back to each country's constitution. In the USA, there is a codified constitution that is entrenched. This means that it is very difficult to change and that it has a different and superior status to other laws and regulations. Sovereignty lies with the US constitution and everything and everyone else is subject to it. This means that the US courts (especially the Supreme Court) have the power to declare the actions of government unconstitutional. In the UK, however, sovereignty is not with a codified constitution, because there isn't one. Here, parliament is sovereign and acts of parliament (statute laws) are the supreme law of the land. Because of this it is impossible for the UK courts to declare laws unconstitutional because once the statute is passed it is, in effect, constitutional.

🄴 The constitution is often a favoured starting-point for this kind of essay and this approach allows the candidate to make a clear and vital point regarding sovereignty and the role of the courts.

In the USA the term 'judicial review' is used to describe the ability of the court to void any actions or statutes, whether by state or federal government, where the court determines that such actions or statutes come into conflict with the constitution. This power was first established in the *Marbury* v. *Madison* case of 1803. Since that time, the Supreme Court has used this power extensively in a broad range of areas.

It is widely accepted that the court has the role of 'guarding' and 'interpreting' the constitution. The court is often asked to make a judgement when disputes arise between states, or between or involving 'public ministers', when state courts disagree, when state courts or state law comes into conflict with federal courts or legislation, or when a state rules out of line with a previous Supreme Court ruling. The court generally has to speak on areas which are the subject of debate or confusion in the lower courts, and such confusion generally arises from areas of the constitution that are more open to interpretation.

While in theory the court is only interpreting the constitution, in practice the differences between interpretations of the same constitutional passage over as short a time as 60 years (e.g. *Plessy* v. *Ferguson* (1896) to *Brown* v. *Board of Education, Topeka* (1954)) may often appear closer to legislative action. Between these two dates the court moved from a position that racial segregation on trains was acceptable (as long as separate accommodation was equal) to ruling that all segregation caused inequality and was, therefore, unconstitutional. Brocker said that the court had 'assumed quasi-legislative authority'.

🄴 This is rather a long section on the USA. Ideally, the style should be more explicitly comparative throughout.

The situation is somewhat different in the UK. With no codified constitution, with parliament sovereign and with statute law supreme, UK courts cannot declare laws unconstitutional. This means that the term 'judicial review' in the UK really refers to the power of the courts to decide whether or not government ministers or government agencies have acted within the powers granted to them in the statute law (*ultra vires*) — rather than whether or not they should have been given such powers in the first place. Even where ministers are found to have acted unlawfully (e.g. Michael Howard), the government can always pass a law through parliament legalising the minister's action retrospectively. The Human Rights Act (HRA), which came into force in 2000, gave the courts the right to declare acts of parliament incompatible with the articles of the HRA but it did not give the courts the right to remove such laws. A declaration of incompatibility just asks parliament to look at things again — without any promise of success. Only when looking at alleged violations of EU law can the courts really force the government to back down (e.g. the *Factortame* case).

> This section shows good understanding of the difference between judicial review in the USA and judicial review in the UK. Some excellent examples help to lend greater authority to the answer.

What we can see, therefore, is that the US judiciary has a good deal more real power than its counterpart in the UK. Whereas the top US court (the Supreme Court) can strike out legislation that violates the constitution, the UK courts can normally only make sure that ministers are doing what the law allows them or tells them to do.

> **This is a strong A-grade response. The candidate understands the nature of sovereignty in the UK and the USA, as well as what this means for the role of the court. The sections dealing with judicial review in each country are very well written.**

Question 12.3

To what extent and by what means have the judiciaries of the UK and the USA become politicised?

(30 minutes)

> An obvious place to start here would be with the appointment process. In both the UK and the USA politicians have traditionally been involved in the appointment process (though at the time of writing the UK government has announced its intention to set up an independent appointments commission). When politicians appoint judges there will always be a danger of politicisation. Another focus of discussion could be the behaviour of the courts and the type of decisions they make. Are they moving beyond the role of 'umpire' towards a situation in which they are effectively 'players', making law through their judgements? In order to deal

with this second point you need to have a good understanding of the position of the judiciary in each country and some examples of cases with which to support your argument.

■ ■ ■

A-grade answer to question 12.3

The word 'politicised' can mean a number of different things. To some people politicisation can occur where politicians have input into the composition or membership of the judiciary, or influence it in such a way as to make it biased in their favour. Politicisation can also refer to a process by which the courts are asked to make political decisions (i.e. decide upon the merit of a law) rather than simply applying the letter of the law. We can deal with each of these two types of politicisation in turn.

🄴 This is an important paragraph. The term 'politicised' might mean different things to different people and the candidate avoids problems later on by setting out at this early stage what he or she understands the term to mean.

At lower levels in the US judiciary, judges are actually elected and this makes them political animals in a sense, because they have to campaign for election and offer the voters a vision of the way in which they intend to apply the law. At the lowest levels of the UK legal system we have unelected magistrates with limited legal training administering justice, so these two systems are very different.

I think that this question is, however, really asking for a focus on the highest-level national courts in each country. In the USA the Supreme Court consists of nine justices who serve a life-long term only ever ended — to date — by incapacity, death or retirement. These justices are appointed by the president of the day when vacancies occur and the president's nominees must be confirmed by majority vote in the Senate. Despite this check by the Senate on the president's power of appointment, many feel that presidents do, in effect, politicise the court through their appointments. Reagan and Bush Senior appointed six out of nine justices to their current positions on the court, including the current chief justice, promoted by Reagan from associate justice in 1986. For many, this is therefore a Republican-leaning court. This is why many were shocked when the court was presented with the opportunity effectively to determine the outcome of the 2000 presidential election, in the midst of the Florida recount débâcle. Some saw its decision in *Bush* v. *Gore* as evidence of the politicisation of the court, though the same could be said of the Florida Supreme Court, which had ordered the recounts to continue in violation of Florida state election laws and the 14th Amendment.

🄴 This is a focused section on the possibility of politicisation through the appointment process, capped off with the obvious example of *Bush* v. *Gore* (2000). What is interesting, however, is that the candidate has avoided simply repeating the commonly reported allegation that the court acted in a biased way by considering the legal basis of the decision made, as well as suggesting possible bias in the Florida Supreme Court.

In the UK, judges have traditionally been appointed by the authority of the monarch but on the advice of the Lord Chancellor, working together with the prime minister. This is clearly a process that could lead to accusations of politicisation. The Lord Chancellor has traditionally been a member of the cabinet (executive), the Lords (legislature) and the head of the judiciary. This fusion of powers has brought increasing criticism in the modern era and Labour's proposals to abolish the role of Lord Chancellor, create a kind of Supreme Court and appoint judges through an independent appointments commission would appear to acknowledge that the danger of politicisation in the current system is real.

e The candidate demonstrates astute awareness of current developments here. The first sentence of the next paragraph is a good linking sentence, allowing the discussion to move on smoothly to the next theme.

More important than judicial composition in raising fears of politicisation is the way in which the high judiciaries of both countries have increasingly been drawn into political debates. In the USA this is hardly a new phenomenon. As early as 1803, in the *Marbury v. Madison* case, the foundations of the power of judicial review were laid down. Nowadays it is accepted that the court has the power to interpret the US constitution, effectively filling in the gaps where the original document is silent (or at least very quiet) or ambiguous. This power has brought the court right into the thick of the political battle. Over black civil rights, the rights of the accused, abortion rights and the freedoms of speech, assembly and religion, the court has ended up effectively 'making law' through its interpretations. Landmark cases such as *Brown* v. *Board of Education, Topeka* and *Roe* v. *Wade* changed American society in a way in which few laws passed through the legislature have.

The situation in the UK has traditionally been very different. The supremacy of statute law and the accompanying sovereignty of parliament have limited even the highest courts. UK courts have not had the power to declare statute unconstitutional because, quite simply, the UK does not have an entrenched constitution against which such statutes can be measured. As a result courts have been limited to the question of whether or not government ministers or government bodies have worked within the statutory guidelines set out or whether they have acted unlawfully. Even when ministers have been caught out (Michael Howard, for example), parliament has often been able to legislate retrospectively to right their wrongs. With the UK's entry into the EEC (from 1973) and its later evolution into the EU, laws are now subject to EU laws and regulations. The *Factortame* case in the European Court of Justice, and House of Lords cases that followed, have shown that courts — even UK courts — can effectively strike down UK legislation if it contradicts EU laws or regulations. The adoption of most of the European Convention of Human Rights through the passing of the Human Rights

Act also gave courts a way of questioning the suitability of certain statutes — though UK courts can only issue a declaration of incompatibility, rather than voiding the offending statute as the US Supreme Court can.

There isn't a formal conclusion here as such. It might be that the candidate simply ran out of time or felt that there was nothing more to say. There is, however, certainly enough here to warrant a grade A.

Civil rights and liberty

Question 13.1

Explain what is meant by the term 'Bill of Rights'.

(10 minutes)

e The term 'Bill of Rights' immediately brings to mind the US Bill of Rights and the danger with this question is, therefore, that you simply write down everything you know about the US Bill of Rights — forgetting that this is a *comparative* question. In order to achieve an A-grade mark here, you need to provide a brief general definition of what a bill of rights is, before moving on to look at the situation in the USA and the UK. Though the UK does not have a formal bill of rights, along US lines, some see the Human Rights Act (HRA) as a step in this direction. The key thing to remember is that the US Bill of Rights is entrenched in a codified constitution whereas the HRA is simply a regular piece of statute law that can be amended and even repealed simply by passing another act of parliament.

■ ■ ■

A-grade answer to question 13.1

A Bill of Rights is a document setting out the basic rights available to the citizens of a nation. In most cases this document is entrenched as part of a codified constitution. As such, the rights contained are very hard to remove.

In the USA the term 'Bill of Rights' refers to the first ten amendments to the US constitution. The Bill of Rights includes the right to freedom of speech and of religion (both 1st Amendment) and the right to bear arms (2nd Amendment), among others. The UK does not have a bill of rights as such. Though there is a document of that name dating back to 1689, it says more about the extent of the monarch's powers than anything else. The closest thing we have to a bill of rights is the Human Rights Act (HRA), which came into force in 2000 and incorporated most of the European Convention of Human Rights into British law. The HRA protects freedom of speech and of religion among other things.

The difference between the HRA and the US Bill of Rights is that the HRA is not entrenched. It can be removed by a simple act of parliament, and even where the courts do use the act to question UK law, all they can do is present a declaration of incompatibility to parliament so that parliament can decide what to do about it. In the USA the Supreme Court can strike down laws that encroach upon the Bill of Rights.

℮ This is a very strong A-grade answer. The candidate provides a clear definition and then puts the term into its US and UK context. The point about entrenchment is a particularly important one.

C/D-grade answer to question 13.1

We use the term 'Bill of Rights' to refer to the first few amendments made to the US constitution. These amendments guarantee a number of basic civil rights, including the freedom of speech. In the USA these rights are very difficult to remove because the only way to do this would be through another constitutional amendment. There is a thing called the Bill of Rights in the UK but it was passed in 1689 and has nearly nothing to do with citizens' rights.

℮ The US material provided here lacks precision. The candidate could refer to the first ten amendments and the example given could also refer to a specific amendment (i.e. the 1st Amendment). The other main weakness is the lack of much comparative material. There is little point in spending much time in discussing the act of 1689 — it would make much more sense to talk about the scope and limitations of the Human Rights Act.

Question 13.2

By what means and how effectively are civil rights protected in the USA and in the UK?

(45 minutes)

℮ One starting-point for this essay could be to explain what you understand by the phrase 'civil rights', as you must identify what kinds of rights you are talking about before you can assess the extent to which they are protected in the UK and the USA. When discussing the USA you should demonstrate a working knowledge of the Bill of Rights (i.e. the first ten amendments to the US constitution). It is important, however, that you acknowledge the fact that US civil rights do not start and end with the Bill of Rights (consider the 13th, 14th and 15th Amendments for example). The work of the US Supreme Court in interpreting these rights requires analysis too. In the UK, you should be able to outline a range of ways in which rights are guaranteed, including the Human Rights Act. Better answers will recognise the way in which the US Bill of Rights and the HRA have different legal status.

A/B-grade answer to question 13.2

One feature common to all liberal democracies is that they offer some protection for the basic civil rights of their citizens. In many countries, including the USA, this protection is achieved through entrenched guarantees included in the country's constitution. In a few countries, including the UK, rights are protected by a combination of traditional principles (common law), acceptable behaviour (the notion of 'reasonableness') and a few key statutes. In order to pass judgement on how effectively the UK and the USA protect their citizens' rights, we must first look at what rights are protected in theory and how this is done before moving on to consider how it works in practice.

e This introduction is focused, but could perhaps do more to explain exactly what we mean by rights. This would make the job of identifying the mechanisms and measures protecting these rights much easier.

The first ten amendments to the US constitution are known collectively as the Bill of Rights. These ten amendments guarantee such basic liberties as the right to freedom of expression and religious belief (both 1st Amendment) and the right to a fair and speedy trial (5th Amendment). These amendments were agreed as part of the deal that saw many states ratify the constitution once it was drafted in 1787. The rights contained therein were aimed at easing the concerns of those states who feared that the new federal government would infringe upon the rights of the individual and that the larger states would dominate the union at a cost to the smaller ones (hence the 10th Amendment). The fact that the USA has a Bill of Rights does not, however, mean that it is not possible to find equally entrenched and fundamental rights set out elsewhere in the constitution. The 13th Amendment, for example, abolished slavery, the 14th guaranteed equal protection under the law and the 26th Amendment gave all US citizens over the age of 18 the right to vote. All of these constitutional provisions, and many more besides, provide a clear body of basic rights and liberties to which all Americans are entitled.

e Many candidates assume, or at least imply, that the Bill of Rights is as far as the USA goes. By recognising the existence of other guarantees, this candidate is already rising above the norm.

The situation in the UK is rather different. In the absence of an entrenched, codified constitution including a Bill of Rights, citizens' rights in the UK are protected by a combination of specific statutes (e.g. the Race Relations Act or any of the various Representation of the People Acts), common law rights and the various treaties and international conventions that the UK has signed up to (such as the European Convention on Human Rights (ECHR)). There is no one place where a UK citizen can look to find all of his or her rights. The closest there is to a US-style Bill of Rights is the Human Rights Act, which makes most of the ECHR articles available to citizens through the British courts. Even this act, however, fails to meet the US benchmark because it is not entrenched and courts can only declare other statutes incompatible where they contradict the HRA — they can't declare them unconstitutional.

☑ The candidate demonstrates very good understanding of the extent and limitations of the Human Rights Act here.

This brings us to the role of the courts. In the USA the constitution (including the Bill of Rights) is sovereign. This means that the US Supreme Court has the power to declare other inferior statutes unconstitutional and therefore void where they go against the constitution. This means that the court has a major role in interpreting the constitution and applying its general principles to the modern age. Whereas the 1st Amendment, for example, protects the 'freedom of speech', the court has taken this to mean not only pure speech (i.e. spoken words) but also non-verbal communication. They call this 'expressive conduct' and activities as varied as burning the US flag and stripping have been judged to fall under its protection. In contrast, the UK courts can do little more than make sure that government ministers and institutions apply the law as it is written. They do not have the power to declare acts of parliament unconstitutional because parliament is sovereign and statute law is supreme.

☑ **This is a very good answer, despite the absence of a clear definition of rights early on. Although the essay is relatively short, it is focused and analytical throughout. It would place it in the A-grade band but probably only at the bottom of the range.**

Elections and voting behaviour

Question 14.1

How significant a role is played by the media in UK and US national elections?

(45 minutes)

e A number of A-level textbooks deal with general media theory in some depth. It is perfectly acceptable for you to bring in this theory when answering a question such as this, but it is important to strike the right balance between theory and practice. The question asks you to comment on the role of the UK and US media in elections in their respective countries. You must, therefore, demonstrate a good knowledge and understanding of the UK and US media in that context as well as a general appreciation of media influence. Above all, you need good illustrative examples.

■ ■ ■

A/B-grade answer to question 14.1

Political scientists on both sides of the Atlantic have often seen the media as having a significant influence on both the course of elections and, in a broader sense, the formation of the political agenda. This essay considers a number of different theories concerning the operation of the media and attempts to assess the extent of media influence in UK and US politics.

e This is a concise introduction, but it effectively sets the direction of the essay.

Some people believe that the mass media are controlled by an elite that uses media with the sole purpose of preserving the status quo and their own position — that they submerge a more radical agenda in meaningless trivia. This is known as 'manipulative theory'. Under this theory, New Labour's re-branding under Blair might have had the effect of making it more acceptable to the dominant elite and, therefore, worthy of support in the face of a divided and unstable Conservative Party. This would explain why media barons such as Rupert Murdoch were prepared to lend their support to Labour after the party abandoned Clause 4. It would also explain why Michael Moore has faced so much criticism from the media. He challenges the 'elite', so he must be discredited.

e The candidate has adopted a theoretical approach, and needs to ensure that plenty of UK and US examples are provided in order to meet the 'comparative' demands of the paper.

This manipulative theory paints quite a negative picture. Hegemonic theory, in contrast, sees the media as less calculating, though just as biased. According to this theory, the people who edit and write in newspapers and those involved in broadcast journalism have a particular view due to their education, age, social class etc. They are bound to write from a particular perspective, however unconscious their bias might be.

Finally, we have the most positive view of the media — pluralist theory. Pluralist theorists hold that there is a range of media output and that individuals choose what to read and watch based on their own outlook and interests. The media therefore reflect opinion rather than shaping it. At best the media probably only reinforce views that readers or viewers have already.

Writers such as the American psychologist Festinger and David Denver have argued that three processes limit media influence. The first is selective exposure. This means that individuals generally choose to expose themselves to newspapers and television programmes that reflect rather than challenge their outlook. The second is selective perception, which occurs when individuals mentally edit the media that they are exposed to, filtering out content that doesn't fit in with their own ideas. Finally, selective retention is the view that people tend to forget programmes and newspaper content that challenge the views that they hold, whilst retaining material that can be used to justify their position.

That said, even Festinger believed that different types of media had different levels of influence. This is because although we view all media output through mental filters, we apply different filters to different types of material. Some argue that television is so powerful because people believe what they see — their filters are effectively down when watching television. When reading newspapers, however, they expect bias and read more carefully.

🄔 Few students are in a position to discuss the works of Festinger and this awareness of media theory would impress an examiner. Ideally, however, there would be some UK and US examples here. The answer is in danger of becoming too theoretical.

Newspapers are not legally required to be impartial and most, if not all, take up clear party positions during election campaigns. The *Sun* was particularly vocal in support of the Conservatives in the 1992 general election, coming up with such memorable headlines as 'Will the last person to leave Britain please turn out the light' when a Labour victory appeared likely. Both Neil Kinnock (the then Labour leader) and Norman Tebbit (a former leading Conservative) believed that the tabloid press had been crucial in contributing to the surprise Conservative victory that year. The *Sun*'s owner, Rupert Murdoch, was courted by New Labour in the run-up to the 1997 general election and the paper eventually backed Labour. Paul Whiteley has estimated that this switch in support cost the Conservatives around 500,000 votes in the election and this might well have made the difference in key marginal seats.

🄔 This is much better. The candidate provides some good UK examples here, but there is still a lack of material covering the USA.

Such open bias is not permitted by the regulations governing television broadcasting. The BBC and the ITC (Independent Television Commission) control broadcasting. Under the terms of the BBC's royal charter and the Television and Broadcasting Acts, the BBC and ITC are supposed to remain politically impartial. This partly reflects the influence credited to broadcast material as opposed to material published in the press. What this impartiality means in practice is that the various channels have to ensure that they are giving fair coverage. They should give the major parties a right to reply when running stories or interviewing ministers and should not give one party or another a disproportionate share of the airtime. Channels are required to provide slots for party political broadcasts too.

This is very different from the USA, where candidates for elected office must buy their own television slots and fund their own television advertising campaigns. The Willie Horton adverts used against Dukakis in 1988 are a good example of the way in which US television is unregulated compared to its UK counterpart.

The candidate demonstrates an excellent awareness of media theory, but the answer would have benefited from being rooted more firmly in UK and US elections. In places, the response reads more like a sociology or psychology essay than a study of politics.

C-grade answer to question 14.1

The media have a major influence on the outcome of elections both in the UK and in the USA. If this were not the case, parties and candidates on either side of the Atlantic would surely not pump such shockingly large amounts of money into managing the media during their campaigns.

In the UK the terrestrial media are controlled quite tightly. Mainstream radio stations and terrestrial television channels are normally required to remain politically neutral. When the BBC news interviews a government minister about a particular policy, therefore, they would normally be expected to ask an opposition spokesman to comment too. This control also extends to advertising time. Parties and candidates in the UK cannot simply buy big chunks of advertising time and flood the screens with adverts. Parties are given limited slots (about 10 minutes at a time) in which they can broadcast their party political messages. UK newspapers are not controlled in the same way and they can have an impact on the course of elections. Newspapers such as the *Sun* were said to have made a difference in the 1992 general election. After that election the *Sun*'s headline ran 'It's the *Sun* wot won it' and in 2001 it used the headline 'It's the *Sun* wot swung it' after switching its support from Conservative to Labour. Neil Kinnock (Labour leader in 1992) and Norman Tebbit (then a leading Tory) also felt that the *Sun* had played a part.

The candidate has a good awareness of the rules governing UK media and brings in some good supporting examples. There could, however, have been more of a focus on the role and importance of the media in shaping the political agenda and influencing voters. A paragraph dealing with media theory would have been helpful early in the essay.

The situation in the USA is slightly different. There are no restrictions on buying television time for political adverts as there are in the UK. In 1992 Ross Perot bought lots of 30-minute peak-time television slots and broadcast lengthy infomercials featuring himself. Though he didn't win, he went from being relatively unknown to being a household name in 12 months and won 19% of the popular vote. In the USA, therefore, television adverts are crucial. Some of these adverts promote a candidate in a positive light, but in recent years there has been a rise in negative, so-called 'attack ads'. These adverts are often funded by extreme pressure groups through Political Action Committees.

Clearly, then, the media play an important role in elections in both the UK and the USA. In the UK, however, the media are regulated far better.

e **There are some good examples here, but the answer is rather short given the 45 minutes available. Though the candidate clearly has some knowledge and understanding, the answer lacks the range and depth of content and analysis required for a higher grade.**

Question 14.2

Why have elections become so candidate-centred on both sides of the Atlantic?

(30 minutes)

e The increasingly candidate-centred nature of elections in the USA has been well reported both in textbooks and in the press — witness Arnold Schwarzenegger's recent candidacy and election as Governor of California. However, few would argue that the situation in the UK is as extreme as that in the USA. This statement, therefore, should not be accepted without qualification. Beyond that, this is another 'what factors'-type question — in this case, 'what factors have led to campaigns becoming so candidate-centred?' To answer successfully you need to identify a range of factors that might have led to the rise of this phenomenon and assess each one in turn.

B-grade answer to question 14.2

There are three reasons why UK and US elections have become so candidate-centred in recent years and these reasons are linked to one another. The first is the decline of political parties. The second is the rise of the modern media — specifically, the medium of television. The third is to do with changes to the electoral system in the last 20 years.

> **e** This is rather a blunt introduction, but it gets the essay moving. Setting out a clear agenda means that the candidate is less likely to become sidetracked and waste what little time is available.

It is not that long since US and UK political parties dominated their respective systems. In the United States, the 1950s and 1960s saw the age of 'machine politics'. Parties were able to tie up political power in certain cities totally. Inside these cities the 'machine' also creamed off the surplus profit from private enterprise. Local 'machine politics' was about the city 'fat cats' in their 'smoke-filled rooms'. In the UK too, the 1950s and 1960s saw a period when the two major political parties took 90% of the public vote at general elections and dominated the political landscape. Elections invariably concerned the party labels rather than the subtle differences between those who wore them. In constituencies across the UK, constituency parties chose candidates whose loyalty to the party was unquestionable. In the USA, states often backed their 'favourite sons' for the big national races every 2 and 4 years. All of this changed, however, in the 1970s and 1980s as the mainstream parties on both sides of the Atlantic went into decline. A number of factors led to this decline.

First, the role which the parties played in terms of providing some kind of 'welfare provision' was undermined by the introduction of national welfare schemes. Changes in the way in which Americans chose their candidates for elected office also led to a focus on the candidate rather than on the party organisation. State initiatives allowed registered voters to bypass the parties and effectively legislate themselves. The rise of primaries over caucuses also undermined the parties' role in candidate selection, in the same way that federal 'matching funds' undermined the role of parties in financing presidential elections.

The media have clearly been responsible, in part at least, for the increasing focus on the candidate over the party and its manifesto. Parties are now often bypassed due to the rise in candidate-centred campaigns. The increasing influence of pressure groups, particularly through their use of Political Action Committees, has also undermined the extent to which candidates can compete financially. All candidates, no matter how modest their campaign, need exposure, which in the USA costs a lot.

For all of these reasons and more, candidates have to fight simply for name recognition and in order to connect with the voter. Even in the UK, candidates who disregard their constituents can find themselves de-selected for the next election, or at least badly positioned to win it. At the same time, we may be witnessing the rise of the independent MP, in light of the election of Martin Bell in 1997 and Richard Taylor in 2001.

> **e** This is a good answer, in which the candidate identifies a number of valid factors and explains each one clearly. However, having set out a clear checklist in the introduction, it would have made sense to deal with the

elements in that order in the body of the essay, rather than jumbling the factors up. The answer is also slightly unbalanced, favouring the USA over the UK. For these reasons, it would be awarded a grade B.

Question 14.3

Critically assess the electoral systems operating in US presidential elections and UK general elections.

(30 minutes)

🄴 To answer this question effectively, you need a good understanding of how each electoral system works. Without this it will be difficult to point out their strengths and weaknesses. As both countries use a form of the first-past-the-post system, a number of strengths and weaknesses are common to them both. It is important to bring in plenty of examples from the UK and the USA so that your answers don't become too generalised and theoretical.

B/C-grade answer to question 14.3

Both the UK and the USA use the first-past-the-post (FPTP) or simple plurality system in their main national elections. In the UK, candidates stand for election in one of the 659 single-member constituencies. The winner in each constituency only requires one vote more than the nearest rival. In the USA too, the FPTP system means that presidential candidates winning a state get all of the Electoral College votes (ECVs) for that state — in all but a handful of cases. This is just one of the aspects of the US system that could be brought into question.

According to Lord Jenkins's Independent Commission on Electoral Reform, an effective electoral system should seek to score highly on four main attributes: proportionality; stable government; voter choice; and the MP–constituency link. It might be helpful to examine the UK and US systems against these markers.

🄴 This is an interesting way into the question. It should certainly allow for a good deal of analysis and prevent the answer from becoming over-descriptive.

Neither the system operating in the UK nor that operating in the USA can claim to offer a great deal of proportionality. As already outlined, the simple winner-takes-all system used on both sides of the Atlantic leads to a situation in which hundreds of thousands of votes are 'wasted' and where, at the extreme, presidents can be elected and the prime minister chosen (on the basis of the numbers of seats won in the Commons) with only a minority of the popular vote. In fact, 1935 was the last year in which the winning party in a UK general election secured more than 50% of the votes cast and in the UK general elections of 1950, 1951 and February 1974 the winning party gained fewer votes nationally than the party that ended up forming the official opposition. The same has occurred in the USA, most recently with the election of George W. Bush, even though he had around 500,000 fewer votes than Gore. The shocking disproportionality of the FPTP system was highlighted most clearly in the 1983 general election, when the Labour Party gained 27.6% of the vote nationally and won 209 seats, whereas the Liberal/SDP Alliance gained 25.4%, yet only won 23 seats.

Second, there is the issue of stable government. Jenkins felt that the FPTP system's main strength was the ability to produce stable governments without the kinds of fragmented legislature common in places such as Israel and, until relatively recently, Italy. This outcome is made possible by the fact that FPTP encourages a two-horse race, thus marginalising third-party candidates. This helps to exaggerate the success of the winning party. Thus, in one of the closest elections ever, Bush won all of the Electoral College votes in Florida and, therefore, passed the 270-vote mark comfortably in the end.

Neither the UK variant of FPTP nor the one operating in the UK provides the voter with a great deal of choice — though we should remember that many US voters at least get the chance to vote in a series of individual FPTP elections on the same day (president, House, Senate, governor etc.).

The MP–constituency link, though well served by FPTP in the UK, is less obvious in the USA. Though House members and Senators must clearly be 'nice' to their constituents, many Congressmen represent impossibly large constituencies (in terms of population). In California, for example, the population is 29 million and there are 53 House members — approximately 550,000 constituents per representative. In the Senate, the situation is even worse, with only two Senators to represent all 29 million Californians. Even in the UK, where the relationship is said to be so crucial, it appears that people are becoming less concerned about being able to talk to their MPs — let alone vote for them.

All in all, it appears that the FPTP system is not particularly effective but that doesn't mean to say that any other system would be any better.

ℯ This is an unorthodox answer, in the sense that it does not really provide much coverage of the actual mechanism. Most candidates would provide some kind of outline early on in order to give context. That said, this candidate demonstrates good knowledge and is able to articulate the ideas within a clearly structured, analytical framework. The response would fall on the borderline between grades B and C.

Political parties

Question 15.1

'It is often said that both the UK and the USA have two-party systems. The reality is rather different, on both sides of the Atlantic.' Discuss.

(45 minutes)

 The first part of the statement is presented as an empirical fact, but it is not. Many commentators argue that neither the USA nor the UK has a true two-party system. It may be more accurate to say that the US and UK party systems have little in common. Again, though, some have argued that the UK system is moving towards that of the USA with parties increasingly becoming less ideological and fighting over the centre ground.

■ ■ ■

A-grade answer to question 15.1

While it is certainly true that the UK and the USA were traditionally said to have 'two-party systems', one could question whether, under close examination, the description can really be applied to either country. At the same time, one might also question the second part of the assessment — whether or not the first part is accurate.

 This is a short but purposeful introduction. The ability to recognise and challenge weaknesses and inferences in this kind of question is one characteristic common to many top A-level students.

At face value, it would appear reasonable to conclude that the USA has a two-party system. Before the 2002 mid-term elections, all but three Congressmen (two House members and one Senator) were from either the Democratic Party or the Republican Party. The two parties dominate the gubernatorial contests (48 out of 50) and the state legislatures similarly, regularly polling over 80% of the popular vote and often over 90% (99% in 1984 and 1988). The last president elected from outside of the two main parties was Martin Fillmore (Whig) in 1850.

Some commentators, however, see things in a rather more subtle way. First, it is clear that competition between the two parties does not happen everywhere: there are still states which always support one party. At the same time, the two main parties are not unified in any ideological sense across the country as a whole. Both parties are broad churches and include within their membership an enormous diversity of attitude and opinion: the words 'Democrat' and 'Republican' disguise a wide range of ideas.

Some writers have gone so far as to say that, rather than a two-party system, the United States in fact has 51 party systems, each unique: one system of parties on a national level in the federal government and another wholly unique party system in each and every one of the 50 states of the Union. Writers such as James McGregor Burns have suggested even more complicated models. In McGregor Burns' model, Republicans from rural areas often have more in common with Democrats from rural areas than they do with their urban Republican colleagues. Democrats from urban areas, in contrast, might align with Republicans from districts facing similar social problems in order to support presidents trying to force through policies that will help these areas. Some commentators have refined this model, using terms such as 'liberal Democrats', 'conservative Democrats', 'moderate 'Republicans' and 'conservative Republicans'.

🄔 This is a rather long US section, which makes some excellent points regarding the nature of the US party system and whether or not the USA even has a two-party system. However, a more explicitly comparative structure is more likely to bring success at the highest level.

The debate over whether or not the UK is truly a two-party system is, if anything, more heated than that over the US party system. Those in favour of the view that the UK is a two-party system point to the fact that the Labour and Conservative parties are the only parties that have a realistic chance of forming a government in the near future or being the senior partner in a coalition. Even in the 2001 general election the Labour and Conservative parties secured 75% of the popular vote and around 90% of the seats in parliament. Despite making progress, the third party (the Liberal Democrats) is still a long way behind the second party (the Conservatives) even when the latter is probably at its lowest ebb.

Some, however, believe that the UK's status as a two-party system ended long ago. They point to the fact that the Labour Party won 246 seats more than the Conservative Party, whereas the Conservative Party only won 114 seats more than the Liberal Democrats. In such a state of affairs, they wonder whether the UK really has two parties capable of winning power. The reality of the situation is that 25% of voters backed a party other than the big two in 2001 and the 90% share of seats won remains artificially exaggerated by the electoral system. Even if the advances made by the Liberal Democrats are still not enough to get people talking about a three-party or multi-party state, we should remember that the party is often second to Labour in the north and west and second to the Conservatives in the south and east. What we might have, therefore, is a series of different two-party systems and some truly multi-party systems. For example, in some Scottish seats there is a genuine four-way race between the Conservative, Labour, Liberal Democrat and Scottish National parties. In addition, it is argued, any party that could mobilise the 41% of the electorate who chose not to vote in 2001 could clearly break the two-party system wide open.

🄔 The candidate provides some good factual information here.

The first part of the statement is, therefore, very contentious indeed — and the second part is equally open to question. UK and US political parties clearly share more than the notion that they are operating in a two-party state. First, both US and UK political parties have become less ideological over the last decade. On both sides of the Atlantic, there has been an obvious effort to position parties in such a way as to gain maximum political advantage while, at the same time, avoiding alienating core voters. Second, both parties have adopted 'third-way-style', mixed-economy approaches to government. Blair's advisors even shared campaigning ideas with Clinton's aides in the run-up to 1997. In fact, since the 1940s Labour has been most commonly compared to the Democrats, whereas Conservatives appear to have more in common with the Republicans. Third, and finally, parties on both sides of the Atlantic are increasingly organisations with limited individual membership. People are simply not joining parties in the same way that they once did.

This candidate takes an extremely direct approach. The introduction and conclusion are both refreshingly 'head-on' and there is plenty of good supporting material.

C/D-grade answer to question 15.1

Although both the UK and the USA have traditionally been seen as two-party systems, there is a lot of evidence to suggest that neither really is.

In the UK, the Liberal Democrats regularly achieve between 15 and 25% of the vote in general elections. They often achieve even better shares of the votes in local elections and in European Parliament elections. The definition of a two-party system is a system where only two parties have a realistic chance of winning an election. In the UK, therefore, we might easily argue that we effectively had a one-party system between 1983 and 1992 (under the Conservatives) and that we currently have a similar situation with Labour. In 1983 the Labour Party and the SDP/Liberal Alliance got roughly the same percentage of the votes available, despite securing vastly different numbers of seats due to our electoral system. After the Brent East by-election, in which the Liberal Democrats came from third to first to unseat Labour, we might be entering into an era where the situation is not totally dominated by two parties. In any case, there are different party systems operating in different parts of the country. In the north, Liberal Democrats are often in competition with Labour, whereas in the southeast it is the Liberal Democrats and the Conservatives who come first and second in many seats. In Scotland, several constituencies are genuine four-way races with the inclusion of the SNP, and the Conservatives won no seats in 1997 so we can hardly talk about a Conservative–Labour two-party system in Scotland, or indeed in Wales, or the southwest.

The same is true in the USA, where parties are very locally based. Republicans from southern states generally have more in common with Democrats from their own states than they do with northern Republicans. This is because the USA is such a varied place. It would be virtually impossible for one unified and ideologically based party to control the whole of the USA. It is true that the two parties control virtually all of the seats in Congress, but this doesn't really mean that much because they are not really parties at all in a national sense; they are just convenient labels.

 There are a number of good points here, but this answer simply does not have the range or the depth required of a higher-grade answer. Another major fault is that it lacks a sense of balance. Rather than advancing a range of arguments for and against the traditional view of the two-party systems, the candidate simply presents arguments that support the quotation in the question.

■ ■ ■

Question 15.2

'Political parties in the UK and in the USA are becoming increasingly irrelevant to the political process.' To what extent would you agree with this assessment?

(45 minutes)

 Although this question appears to be focused on political parties, you need to look at more than parties alone if you are to achieve a top grade. If we are to judge political parties as increasingly irrelevant, then we must also explain why this might be so. One way of approaching this question would be to see it as a question about changing styles of political participation. A lot has been said in recent years about the decline of political parties and the rise of pressure groups and direct action campaigns. A number of commentators have also written of an 'end of ideology' as political parties race towards the centre ground, abandoning their core voters. Both of these trends could feature in your answer.

■ ■ ■

A-grade answer to question 15.2

In recent years many political commentators have commented on what they have seen as a rise in political apathy. This apathy is most evident, it is argued, in low voter turnout on both sides of the Atlantic and in falling individual membership of mainstream political parties. Some, however, have argued that this is not evidence of political apathy but simply a sign that people have moved on — that they are still participating, but simply doing so in different ways. This means that, as the title suggests, political parties have just become 'increasingly irrelevant to the political process'.

 This is an interesting way of tackling the question. Political apathy and disaffection is a topic that many students will have studied. While it is dangerous to attempt to turn an essay into something that it is not, the approach taken here is perfectly valid. The introduction, though not setting out a clear agenda, does put the issue firmly into context.

During the 1950s and 1960s, in the UK and in the USA, levels of partisan alignment were high. The big political parties in both countries dominated the political landscape and controlled political power. Party membership, in the UK at least, was in the millions during this period and it really seemed to matter which of the parties you voted for because they stood for something. In the USA, the Democrats were seen as the more liberal party. They had become associated with the tax-and-spend policies of the New Deal and could be relied upon to increase welfare spending. The Republicans, in contrast, were conservative, favouring smaller government, lower taxes and the right of state governments to manage their own affairs. In the UK the situation was similar. The Labour Party, formed by the socialist societies and the unions, was wedded to the idea of redistributing wealth. Clause 4 was a kind of mission statement for the party. The Conservatives, in contrast, represented those on middle and higher incomes. Parties at this time, even in the USA, were more ideological than they have become today.

Candidates often get 'bogged down' in lengthy historical narratives. Here, however, the student keeps the background material fairly concise and focused.

What has happened in recent years is that society has changed. Fewer people in the UK and the USA are in absolute poverty and most people have come to view capitalism in its modern form as basically acceptable. This has meant that more left-wing parties such as 'old' Labour in the UK and the more 'liberal' Democrats in the USA have had to adapt their policies accordingly. This in turn has led parties into a massive rush towards middle England and middle America. Parties have abandoned some of their core principles and traditions in the chase for votes. As a result, many people have found it difficult to distinguish between the main political parties on offer. Some feel that this has led to voter apathy, and it probably has. What it has also done, however, is to push people out into other forms of political activity.

It is no coincidence that pressure groups and direct action campaigns have multiplied as political parties have declined. Greenpeace UK now has more members than the Conservative Party and it is difficult to imagine a situation in which any UK political party could get hundreds of thousands of people to march to London, as we have seen in recent years with the Countryside Alliance marches and the 'Stop the War' campaign. People are simply voting with their feet and beginning to work outside the normal channels. By the normal channels I mean voting for MPs, writing letters and such like. Nowadays, people in the UK have come to the conclusion that MPs listen more to their party whips than to their constituents, so they turn to pressure group activity and direct action in order to get their message across. In the USA, the feeling that the democratic process is failing has led to a rise in extreme and in some cases violent direct action. Anti-abortionists, for example, have bombed abortion clinics and murdered surgeons.

e This is drifting towards an answer on political culture/political participation, but the paragraph is not out of place in this essay, given the discussion immediately preceding it.

In conclusion, it is clear that for many UK and US citizens political parties no longer provide a sufficiently convincing way of participating in the political process. In that sense they have become irrelevant. Obviously, they are still relevant in the sense that they win most elections and control the government institutions in both countries, but they are increasingly irrelevant to the people and, if they continue to be so, we are likely to see an increasingly unstable form of single-issue direct action democracy, as opposed to the representative democracy with which we have been familiar in past decades.

e **A considered and effective conclusion rounds off a well-thought-out and focused survey. The candidate clearly understands the issues central to this question and is able to see changes in the nature of political parties within their broader contexts. This is an A-grade response.**

Pressure groups

Question 16.1

'The USA is far more suited to pressure group activity than the UK due to the nature of American society and the system of government set out under its constitution.' How accurate is this view?

(45 minutes)

e It is certainly true that the nature of a particular society and the structure of its system of government has a bearing on the relative influence of parties and pressure groups. You need to identify the essential differences between UK and US society and between the UK and US systems of government. This will enable you to show how differences between the UK and the USA favour pressure groups over political parties, or vice versa.

■ ■ ■

A-grade answer to question 16.1

The relative role and importance of political parties and pressure groups within any country is determined by two key factors: the nature of that society; and the structure of its political system.

e This is not really a paragraph. If you are pushed for time, you may be forced into this kind of truncated introduction, but it is always better to produce a proper introductory *paragraph* — even if it is a short one.

The United States is a heterogeneous society — that is to say, it is massively varied in terms of population (ethnicity, religion, culture etc.), geographically, climatically and economically. There are, in fact, so many different interests that parties cannot possibly hope to encompass them all effectively. In this context, pressure groups flourish and proliferate. National political parties, in contrast, tend to be very 'broad churches' — or 'big umbrellas', as some prefer to put it. They attempt to put together as broad a coalition of voters as possible in order to secure control in Washington, but are less important between presidential elections.

The UK, in contrast, is a smaller country. Political parties have traditionally been able to remain meaningful and ideological whilst still being elected. UK political culture has traditionally been characterised by homogeneity, deference and consensus. People have tended to be less keen to get involved in pressure groups and direct action. They put their faith in those who know best and trust the government.

The structure of the US government both reflects the diversity in US society and reinforces it. As Alexander Hamilton noted, the constitution aimed to establish a system of government in which 'no alliance of interests could ever gain control of the whole'. The constitution brought about a fragmentation of power in a number of ways. First, it included a separation of powers between legislative, executive and judicial branches. Second, it established checks and balances. Finally, it split government up between federal and state governments. These three features of the US constitution fragmented power and this fragmentation presents pressure groups with numerous points of leverage. For example, they can exert pressure at federal or state level or on any or all of the branches of government.

 If you are going to use quotations, they need to be short, memorable, relevant and authoritative. Hamilton's remark is, therefore, the type of example you should follow.

In the UK, the situation is very different. The UK has an incomplete separation of powers. Lord Hailsham once described the UK as an 'elective dictatorship' because the sovereign parliament could be dominated wholly by majority party, government, cabinet and prime minister. The UK is also a unitary state, despite the recent devolution schemes. This concentration of power at Westminster makes it more difficult for pressure groups to exert leverage. There are fewer access points than in the US political system and this makes it far more difficult for pressure groups to operate effectively.

 The point about the incomplete separation of powers is a good one; most candidates refer to the UK as having no separation of powers.

It is true, therefore, that the USA is more suited to pressure group activity for the reasons given. Having said that, the situation in the UK is starting to change. People are now less deferential than they once were and we have seen an end to homogeneity and consensus. Political parties in the UK are becoming less ideological and more similar as they fight for the votes of 'middle England'. As a result, more people are now turning to pressure group activity because they are becoming disillusioned with the parties. There are also more points of leverage than there used to be because of greater EU integration and the devolution of power to Scotland, Northern Ireland, Wales and, soon, to the regions.

 This answer's strength is that it provides a sound theoretical framework early on: that is, the idea that everything depends upon the nature of society and associated political structures. This framework allows the candidate to move through the survey in a coherent and logical fashion. Although it is shorter than many answers at this level, and the introductory paragraph could have been improved, this response would gain a grade A.

Question 16.2

In both the USA and the UK the nature of political participation is changing: fewer people are voting and joining political parties; more are becoming involved in pressure group activity and direct action campaigns. Why might this be the case and what consequences might this shift in participation bring for governments in both countries?

(45 minutes)

 The A-grade answer to question 15.2 reveals how a question focusing on the decline of parties could end up being a question on changing trends in participation — in part at least. This question, in contrast, focuses explicitly on the question of political participation. Many of the points made in the advice for question 15.2 apply here too. It is also important, however, that you look beyond the statement in the question, to the question itself. The question falls, in effect, into two parts: first, you are asked to identify why these changes might be happening; and second, you must try to look beyond these changes to consider their possible mid- to long-term consequences.

A-grade answer to question 16.2

Studies of political participation often rightly focus on levels of voter turnout. It is, however, important to remember that there are other forms of political participation, not least involvement in political parties and pressure group activity, as the title suggests.

 This introduction does not set out a clear agenda but at least provides an idea of the scope of the discussion ahead.

One of the most obvious ways in which an individual can participate within a political system is to vote. Turnout rates are, therefore, one important measure of political participation. Low voter turnout in the 2001 general election (59%) caused widespread concern in the UK, and the USA has a long history of similarly low turnouts and low voter registration rates. Why have people turned away from voting on both sides of the Atlantic?

Some argue that low turnout is a reflection of how important a given election is. Put simply, voters are more likely to turn out to vote when they can see that the resulting institutions are important. This explains why many voters who vote in general elections do not bother to vote in local elections or EU elections. In 1999 the overall national turnout for UK elections to the European Parliament was only 24%. This was the lowest for any EU member state. In the 2000 local government elections, turnout was around

25%. Regional government elections were also shunned by the voters. In Scotland 59% of voters turned out, in Wales only 40% voted and in London the turnout for the GLA elections was just 32%. US voters have been similarly reluctant. In the presidential election of 2000, turnout was 51.3%, whereas in the mid-term elections in 1998 the figure was 36%. Some voters clearly cannot be bothered to vote, however important the election is.

e The candidate makes a sophisticated point about differential turnout and provides excellent examples to illustrate this.

Increasing numbers of voters are coming to the conclusion that elections do not matter. All parties are the same and it is more profitable to spend time engaged in direct action on single issues — as the title suggests. It is interesting that one of the seats with the best turnout in the 2001 UK general election was in Wyre Forrest, where the independent Dr Richard Taylor won on a 75% turnout by running what was essentially a single-issue pressure group campaign aimed at saving a hospital.

e This is another excellent point. Though many candidates might refer to the low turnout, few would have the necessary knowledge and understanding to make such a subtle point.

People are increasingly seeing political parties as an irrelevance. The two parties appear to have moved together in recent years and neither really has much of an ideological core any more. People have a sense that parties are just chasing after the votes of middle England and that policy won't change much, whoever they elect. This has resulted in a significant falling off not only of voting but also of people actually joining political parties.

The fact that fewer people are voting and that the membership of most political parties is significantly lower than it was in the 1950s does not, however, mean that people are not participating in other ways. In the *Independent*, Noreena Hertz was quick to point out that 'it's not about apathy...while voting is waning, other forms of political expression are on the rise'. Though she was commenting on the UK, the USA is experiencing a similar trend.

e A good point is made in the first sentence of the last paragraph, though you should avoid double negatives. They make the argument more difficult to scan and take on board.

The membership of mainstream pressure groups such as Greenpeace has risen as the membership of the major political parties has fallen. Greenpeace's membership rose from 30,000 in 1981 to over 400,000 in 1992, whereas the Conservative Party's membership fell from 2.8 million in the 1950s to 780,000 in 1992 and 335,000 by the end of 2000. There has also been a marked increase in direct action (e.g. anti-roads campaigners, fuel protesters). The same can be said of the USA, with a rise in — for example — direct action anti-abortion campaigns.

Such developments may not be a good sign on either side of the Atlantic. Though public participation in politics should be welcomed, the massive increase in direct action campaigns undermines the principles of a representative democracy. The people who work on the modern political extremes are people who would have been within mainstream political parties in the 1970s, before the major parties all made a beeline for the centre.

e **This is an effective conclusion. It draws the earlier discussion together and makes a sophisticated point regarding what this change in participation might mean for representative democracy. This would be a solid A-grade response.**

■ ■ ■

D-grade answer to question 16.2

Far fewer people now join political parties than they once did. In the UK the Conservative Party and the Labour Party only have around 300,000 individual members each and the Liberal Democrats only have around 100,000. That means that out of a total population of around 60 million, only 700,000 can be bothered to join political parties.

One reason why party membership might be so low is political apathy. Many people are just not interested in politics any more. But this ignores the fact that people are getting involved in other types of political activities. The title, for example, talks about the rise of pressure groups and direct action campaigns. The Royal Society for the Protection of Birds (RSPB) now has over 1,000,000 members — more than all UK political parties put together. Greenpeace has over 300,000 UK members — the same as the Conservatives — and hundreds of thousands of people have gone on marches organised by groups such as the Countryside Alliance and the 'Stop the War' campaign. At the same time, the average age of Conservative Party members is said to be over 60 and the average age of those who attend the Conservative Party conference is said to be nearly 70.

People still participate politically but they choose not to do it through political parties. This is because they do not see political parties as institutions through which they can achieve their goals. Many young people feel that a conservative, middle-class, middle-aged, white elite dominates political parties — and they are probably right. Young people are looking for results that are a little more immediate, so they tend to favour forms of participation that will give them that. The various anti-roads protesters in the 1990s ('Swampy' and the others) had a real impact in that they made highway construction so expensive that it made the government think again. The fuel protests of 2000 also forced the government to climb down over fuel duty. The anti-live animal export campaigns of the 1990s were successful too, as were the anti-Poll Tax campaigns. In all of these examples, direct action or pressure group action brought about fairly rapid results where traditional methods had failed to stop a government with a strong majority. This is one reason why people are abandoning political parties in favour of other forms of participation in the UK. Another reason is that the UK parties are too similar to one another. They will say anything to get elected and seem to be obsessed by 'middle England'. As a result, those people who are not in 'middle England' feel left out and look to other methods.

In the USA, political parties have always been fairly meaningless. There are more differences within the parties than there are between them. US parties, even more than their UK counterparts, are obsessed by a need not to offend anyone. As a result, anyone with any goals that are not universal to everyone will probably have to pursue them through pressure groups rather than through parties. The USA has also seen a rise in more extreme and violent pressure groups as people become disillusioned even by normal pressure group activity. This has been particularly common over issues such as abortion.

The candidate shows some understanding of the key issues, but needs to do rather more to impose a structure on the discussion. There are some excellent examples here but they need to be incorporated into a more convincing analytical framework rather than just being listed as they are in places. The lack of a conclusion merely highlights the candidate's failure to plan the answer before starting. The comparative element of the answer is affected by this lack of planning too. The US section is far too brief compared to the UK section.